Travel with Children

Children

Maureen Wheeler

Travel with Children - a travel survival kit
  2nd edition

Published by
  Lonely Planet Publications
  Head Office: PO Box 617, Hawthorn, Vic 3122, Australia
  US Office: PO Box 2001A, Berkeley, CA 94702, USA

Printed by
  Colorcraft Ltd, Hong Kong

Photographs by
  Tony Wheeler (TW)
  Lesley O'Donnell: Portrait of Maureen & children (p3)
  Front cover: Off Lamu, Kenya (TW)
  Back cover: Snorkelling off outrigger, Bali, Indonesia (TW)

First Published
  May 1985

This Edition
  April 1990

National Library of Australia Cataloguing in Publication Data

Wheeler, Maureen.
  Travel with children.

  2nd ed.
  Includes index.
  ISBN 0 86442 075 7.

  1. Travel – Health aspects – Asia. 2. Children – Care and hygiene – Asia.
  3. Asia – Description and travel – 1951 –   – Guide-books. I. Title

613.68083

text © Maureen Wheeler 1990
photos © photographers as indicated 1990

Maureen Wheeler

Maureen Wheeler was born in Belfast, Northern Ireland. At age 20 she moved to the 'big city' – London, where three days later she met Tony Wheeler on a park bench in Regents Park. They were married a year later and set off to see the world, ending up in Australia. In 1974 they established Lonely Planet Publications – since then Maureen and Tony have written many travel guides and published many more. In between trips, Maureen completed a degree in social work but faced with a choice between a career and travelling, chose to make travel her career. Their children, Tashi and Kieran, accompany Maureen and Tony on their frequent travels and considerably enliven the experience.

About this Book

For many people of my generation travel as children was most likely to be a visit to grandma, or a week or two at a not too far distant beach. Few children travelled 'abroad' with their parents (actually comparatively few parents travelled abroad). Nowadays that has changed considerably; many of the people who are now parents spent a lot of time travelling in the '60's and '70's, exploring places that to their parents were only names in a song or movie.

The trails across Asia, Africa and South America which were once peopled by young, curious westerners now carry the same people, just older and wiser (?). The trips are shorter due to the waiting jobs, but the curiosity is still strong, and more and more often these travellers are accompanied by their young children.

Since I fit right into the above description, I decided to write this book having been asked for information many times by parents who are wondering if travel will have to be postponed until the children are older, or if it is possible when the children are young.

For Tony and I, travel is our business and an integral part of our lives, so the question of 'whether' did not arise, just the question of 'how'.

Lonely Planet Credits

Editor	Katie Cody
Cover design, design and illustrations	Trudi Canavan

A Request

Because every family is different, your experiences of travel with children will vary from ours. So if you find things better or worse than we suggested, please write and tell us and help make the next edition better!

Your letters will be used to help update future editions and, where possible, important changes will also be included as a Stop Press section in reprints.

All information is greatly appreciated and the best letters will receive a free copy of the next edition, or any other Lonely Planet book of your choice.

Contents

INTRODUCTION Why Travel With Children?   7

TRAVEL WITH CHILDREN Pre-Departure Preparation – Passports –   9
Visas – On The Road With Children – Rules of the Road – Childish
Things To Do – People – Local Children – Culture – Culture Shock –
Babysitters – Money – Involve Them –

TRAVELLERS' TALES The Australian Outback – New Zealand –   26
Cook Islands

GETTING THERE & AROUND Flying – Fares & Baggage   35
Allowance – Service – Airports – What To Bring – Food – Sleeping –
Where to Sit – Medication – Preparation for the Flight – Motion
Sickness – What to Wear on the Flight – Take-off (& Landing) –
Changing Time Zones – Other Transport – Long Distance –
Rent-a-Cars – Local Transport – Bicycles – Strollers & Backpacks –
Walking & Trekking

TRAVELLERS' TALES Bali – Indonesia – Nepal, India & Sri Lanka   61

ON THE ROAD What To Take – Clothes – Hotels & Sleeping –   69
Cribs/Cots – What to Carry for Sleeping – Bathing – Toilets – Food –
Breast Feeding – Solid Food – Drinking – Where You Eat –
Alternatives – Food Rules – Things to Bring for Eating

TRAVELLERS' TALES Japan, Hong Kong & Macau – Japan – China   91

HEALTH Travel Health Guides – Pre- Departure Preparations –   104
Basic Rules – Medical Problems & Treatment – Fever – Climatic
& Geographical Considerations – Diseases of Insanitation – Diseases
Spread by People & Animals – Insect Borne Diseases – Cuts, Bites
& Stings

TRAVELLERS' TALES South America – Mexico   133

TRAVELLING PREGNANT When to Travel – Be Prepared –   138
Food – Supplements – Other Considerations – Travel Health –
Vaccinations – Diarrhoea – Malaria – Minor Problems

TRAVELLERS' TALES Africa   143

INDEX   152

Introduction

WHY TRAVEL WITH CHILDREN?

Tony and I have travelled ever since we first met in the early '70s. Although at times families and friends have had occasion to worry about our choice of destination, or method of getting there, on the whole most people seemed to agree that travel was beneficial and we were very lucky to do so much. Knowing how much travel was a part of our lives, not to mention our livelihood, those same families and friends were quite surprised when we added children to the equation, deeming it quite impossible to continue travelling in the areas we did, with children.

When Tashi was six months old, we went on a trip around Malaysia, Singapore, England and Ireland, the USA and back to Australia. We travelled for five months and discovered that it was a totally new experience with a child, but still rewarding. Two years later her brother Kieran joined us and he took his first real trip, to the island of Bali, when he was four months old. Before his first birthday he had also been to Thailand, Nepal, India and Sri Lanka. Our children are now eight and six years of age and with them we have made trips to Canada and the USA in North America; to Mexico and several of the Andean countries in Latin America; to a number of Pacific Islands; to New Zealand and Australia (of course); to Japan, Hong Kong and Macau in North-East Asia; to Indonesia, Singapore, Malaysia and Thailand in South-East Asia; to Nepal, India and Sri Lanka on the sub-continent; to Kenya and Zimbabwe in Africa; and to England and Ireland in Britain.

So travel with children is possible, but why bother? Well if travelling is one of your major pleasure in life, why stop? Children can increase the hassles in travel, but they can also make it even more fun. Tony and I have taken Tashi and Kieran to places we had visited before, and have found that it is a new experience with them in tow. We meet more local people: parenthood is universal so we immediately have something in common with most people we meet. The experience is fascinating for us and the children enjoy it and benefit immensely from meeting other people and playing with their children.

The problems exist of course. How you travel and where you stay and eat all have to be considered more carefully when you have children with you, and more care has to be taken to ensure the children stay healthy. It can be tiring; there will be times when you feel hot, dusty and fed up after a long trip, or you may have had a particularly hassling day and you badly need some peace and quiet, and then there's junior also hassled, also fed up and you're supposed to do something. At times you wish you had listened to all the good advice and stayed home; however, I'm writing this book for all the dedicated travellers who feel that to stay home, or to limit travel to the safest, easiest options 'because of the children' is to deny yourself and your children the most fantastic experience you can have, the best adventures and the best opportunity to learn about the world.

Travel with Children

PRE-DEPARTURE PREPARATION

You can help prepare your children for the trip. A month or so beforehand it is a good idea to get as much literature as you can on the area you are going to. Get tourist literature, books from the library– anything with pictures. Try to find books of legends or children's stories from the region. Tashi first encountered the Hindu story of Rama and Sita from the Ramayana in Bali, loved the story and was enthralled to see pictures depicting the story carved on temple walls, or danced at local festivals. Allusions to it pop up all over South-East Asia and the sub-continent.

For a month to six weeks before we leave home, we read stories about the places we are going to. Even if it isn't really a story, a travel brochure can be made to seem like one, just by explaining the pictures. You may be surprised at how much sticks.

In Nepal Tashi pointed out the ladies carrying things on their heads and said 'just like in the book' – many things she was delighted to find were 'just like in the book'. You can also start taking your children out to eat in restaurants, going for trips, taking them for walks – in short preparing them for travelling. Try introducing different foods or flavours into your cooking – not too many, most children will recoil on principle when anything new is offered, but they will sometimes try new food in a new country when it is served up in a restaurant. Include your children in your planning, ask what they want to bring, ask them to select the books they would like to have with them. I usually buy a few new books which I produce when we are packing.

As soon as our children were able to walk, they were given their own little daypacks to take on the plane with them. In it are their books and a few toys and I usually try to have a few surprise books and games for them to find on the plane. You do have to make it

clear that it is their pack and they must (when possible!) carry it, so keep it light.

Passports

In most countries, a parent can have any children added to their own passport. The fee for this, if there is one, will be less than for getting a separate passports for the children, but the drawback is that the children can only travel with that one parent. If the children are in the mother's passport and for some reason the mother has to return home the children must accompany her. In the case of very small children that would probably happen anyway, but where they are older it may be a nuisance. Another hassle may be that the father may want to take the children somewhere without the mother; again this would not be possible unless they had their own passports.

On the other hand, apart from the additional expense, if your children have their own passports, the photographs could show gorgeous, bald, toothless babies which may not please them when they are, say, five. To change the photo is more bureaucracy and money. Separate passports also mean that you have that little bit more to carry and take care of (passports are often coveted by the unscrupulous element present in every country).

Tony and I opted for the children going on my passport at first but now they have passports of their own.

Visas
Children usually require visas just like adults and there don't seem to be any reduced rates. If the children are included on the parent's passport, separate visas still have to be stamped for the children.

ON THE ROAD WITH CHILDREN
The age of your children is an important factor in how you travel. Babies are portable, don't have too many preferences for what they see or do, but do require a lot of equipment – nappies, changes of clothes, special implements – and do need some kind of routine for naps, feeding and changing. They may also get you up at night, and in a hotel room that may not go down too well with neighbours. There is also more anxiety with babies on the move; they can't tell you if they are too hot, too cold, or get a stomachache. And as parents are at their most anxious with small babies, travelling probably exacerbates that anxiety. On the plus side babies are easy to entertain and you can take them anywhere – a day in a museum is a possibility with a baby in a backpack or stroller – plus you get to dictate where you go and what you do. This is probably the only stage of their lives you can!

Toddlers are probably the most difficult; all that energy and trying-to-do-everything and all the frustrations of not being allowed to. The plus side is the interest toddlers bring to everything, the down side is having to watch them every minute and chase them to bring them back when they go too far. Also, toddlers are fussy eaters and obstinate in their likes and dislikes.

From about four years on, travel with children becomes a real pleasure. It is still hard work, but also very rewarding as your children now form their own impressions and relationships, and can tell you what they are experiencing. As your children get older they will tell you what they enjoy and planning trips will be more of a group effort with their likes and dislikes being taken into account, within reason (how many times can you do Disneyland after all?).

Rules of the Road

Some children may love all day bus trips, or three day train journeys through India, or visiting museums and art galleries for hours on end, but I wouldn't count on being the parent of such children. Many children, however, will enjoy all of these things in child-sized doses.

There are occasions when an all day bus trip is necessary and an overnight trip on a train with a sleeper may be very exciting, but three days on a train is excessive for any child's endurance level, so maybe the Trans-Siberian should wait until your children are old enough to decide that this is how they want to spend their vacation.

Museums can be fascinating, as can ruined cities and ancient buildings: Tashi and Kieran thought Macchu Picchu was great – a terrific place for a game of hide and seek! The superb Anthropological Museum in Mexico City may have had only limited child-appeal itself but the fountains and pond outside kept them happy for quite a while while we browsed. Most things you want to do while travelling will have some appeal for children even if not in quite the way you thought.

There are various strategies you can employ to keep everyone happy. With very young children you may decide you would enjoy a gallery visit more if you went solo, so parents can split up; one stays with the child and one visits the museum, and next day vice-versa. Some travelling parents take it in turns to have one day off each week. This may be the day when you wander around, stopping for cold drinks or snacks wherever takes your fancy, browsing through shops or talking to other travellers, or just lazing on the beach reading a book, savouring the fact that there are no interruptions. Some people find this works very well, giving each parent a safety valve.

When your children are a bit older they may well accept the 'turns' system. You explain to them that you want to visit a museum in the morning, but in the afternoon they get to choose what they want to do, whether it is playing in their room, shopping for presents for friends, going to a playpark or swimming pool or whatever. If you do have a day on a bus, make the next day an 'at ease' day, when you all relax and the children get to choose the activities.

Young children get very tired and, like everyone else, cope less well with life when they are. Trying to avoid overtiring your children is easier said than done, but try to structure your day around their needs. Think about what you want to do and then how best to do it. If it requires a fairly long bus trip to get to some attraction, then perhaps the morning is the best time, when they are fresh and cheerful, and the ride back may be a good time to have a sleep. Children rarely do things to plan, but knowing your children will give you some clues on how to structure things.

Don't fill your days with things to do, children need some unstructured play time in each day. Take a few hours each day to retire to your hotel and let them put in a few hours as they please – whether it is playing with toys, drawing, reading being read to or whatever.

Where possible, choose places to stay with your children in mind. Any kind of garden, verandah, or just space which is near your room and is safe, is worth having. A swimming pool is top of the desirable facilities; my two can spend hours jumping in and splashing around and after a hot sticky morning of city-seeing it seems like heaven. A hotel room in itself is not a very stimulating environment, but being able to sit on a verandah and watch people going about their business, or run around a small patch of garden chasing a butterfly, may just be the difference between being able to relax and let go for a while and feeling trapped and frustrated. At one hotel in Bali Tashi became very friendly with the gardener and used to follow him around 'helping' with his work; she loved it and he seemed pleased by her devotion.

Allow your children to experience things in their own way. The

Buddha statue may seem very impressive to you, but if your son seems to be more interested in the vendor of sticky drinks, don't think the trip is a failure and your little philistine would have been better at home. You'll be surprised at the memories he will take home, and often quite unprepared for the insights he will have of the culture and people he met. Don't devalue the things your children find exciting and wonderful or try to always turn their attention to what you feel is a more important aspect of what you are seeing. So long as they find something exciting and wonderful the trip will be a success.

Childish Things To Do

Just about everywhere you can find things that seem to be tailor-made for children. Children are fascinated by the obvious differences from life back at home – the houses people live in, the forms of transport (horsecarts, rickshaws, crowded buses or whatever), the way people dress and the local customs will all provide interest for your child.

There are special things which may be interesting to anyone but are especially thrilling for children. The elephant school in north Thailand, kite flying on the east coast of Malaysia, the bat cave in Bali, and wildlife almost anywhere, all have a special fascination for children.

Equally there are things that adults might well pass by but which prove absolutely irresistible to children. We visited a small town fun fair in Ecuador that may have paled beside Santa Cruz or Luna Park but was just fine for two small kids. Dunia Fantasi in Jakarta, a pretty good attempt at a sort of Asian Disneyland, was one of the high spots of a visit to Java. The Tiger Balm gardens in Singapore and Hong Kong are deliciously terrifying and even the grottiest little local aquarium will be of some interest. Markets are generally pretty exciting wherever they are and children will window shop anywhere.

There are plenty of strictly-for-children attractions all over the world and it's fascinating to see how they are often much the same as back home. We've tried out local playparks from India to

Ecuador or Bolivia to Zimbabwe and a visit to the numerous temples in Japan's temple city of Kyoto was interspersed with trying out the slides and swings in tiny Japanese playgrounds.

Besides all the special treats and strictly-for-children attractions, don't underestimate their ability to be awed, enchanted and delighted by more 'cultural' pursuits. Stories of the legends behind the temple sculptures, the rituals enacted each day at religious ceremonies, and the local festivals can all be explained simply – even to a very young child. On a visit to Kathmandu our early morning walk to breakfast was always full of excitement and interest. We saw the markets being set up, the man spinning clay into little *chai* (tea) cups, a cow stealing vegetables from a stall, all before our morning bowl of muesli! Tashi was also most impressed by Kathmandu's Black Bhairab statue. We were told that naughty children were taken here and shown this fearsome statue to encourage them to reform. Tashi was certainly thoughtful for a while after hearing this story and seeing the fearful image!

Away from our familiar environment things aren't always quite the way they seem. A glass-bottom boat trip to view the coral in Sri Lanka turned out to be hanging over the edge of a dugout canoe to look into a glass-bottomed box. I sat perched on the edge of the canoe, feet trailing in the water with a rather worried eight-month-old Kieran clutched to me. Four years later, on another canoe off another coral reef (this time in Bali), he would happily leap into the water and hang on to the outrigger between dives.

People

The people will be the most important memories your children will take home and you will be surprised at how many they remember. In many countries tourism is definitely a two way thing and often you are the centre of attention. There must be hundreds of photographs of my children adorning the shelves in homes all over the world. It's often commented on how the Japanese love to be photographed in front of the local sightseeing attraction. It's an equally popular activity for many other nationalities, but even better is to be photographed in front of the local temple standing

next to a foreigner – your children are often simply 'borrowed' to complete the photo!

The interest in your child can sometimes be negative – many Asians consider children communal property and are used to handing their own children around from person to person, to admire and cuddle. They will expect to do the same with yours and up to a point this may be fine, but your child will soon protest when it starts to happen every few minutes. A single pinch on the cheek may be OK but 15 or 20 in as many minutes hurts! Gales of laughter if your child shrieks in protest or even bursts into tears don't help either.

Some parents feel their children should learn to cope with this, that it is part of the culture you are travelling in and it is therefore rude to refuse to be part of it. You have to make your own decisions how to handle it but I tend to try and protect the children from it as much as possible, I wouldn't like being grabbed by a dozen strangers either! I let the children set their own limits and back them up. I don't try to coax them into being nice to people they don't want to be nice to, although I don't encourage rudeness of course. Children are a curiosity and are made to feel one, which is unsettling for most people, let alone a small child. If I get questioning looks when my children irritably brushes away an unwanted hand or resolutely turns their back on someone trying to pick them up, I just smile sympathetically, shrug my shoulders and pick them up or put an arm around them. One way to deal with the problem is to put your children out of reach of curious hands; Tashi loved riding on Tony's shoulders for that reason.

Local Children

One of the nicest aspects of travelling with young children is that, no matter where you are or what the language is, your child will make friends and communicate beautifully with the local children. In many places older children can be trusted to be responsible for your child if they all go off wandering.

As they get older, children tend to need to have a common language before they can really play together for any length of time. Even a little can go a long way but we find that our children are frustrated when they can't communicate with other local children so the relationships they strike up now are generally with the children of other travellers. If you do find yourself staying at a hotel where there is another family with children of a similar age you will generally feel you've struck oil – the children will be so delighted to have other children to play with and communicate with that you may not see them from one meal to the next and both sets of parents can act as alternate child minders so everyone gets a break. Lunch à deux can seem wonderful if every meal for the last month has been a family one.

Despite the difficulties in communicating children do notice each other and study each others' behaviour. It is interesting to discover what your children are noticing and what they think of it. The beach is a good place to observe cultural differences and also one of the few places where your children can engage in a noisy, boisterous game with the local children and not require too much spoken communication. In many places, in Asia in particular, people come along the beach to sell things and will often sit down for a chat if you have children. Their English may be limited but it can be a good opportunity for a mutual language lesson.

One thing to be aware of on the beach, however, is that many local children are not taught to swim and are not very proficient in the water, although they may splash around happily in the shallows. Swimming as a recreational sport is not widely practised in many under developed countries – often the fishermen who go far out to sea in little sailing boats cannot swim. If your children are good swimmers and are playing with local children you have a responsibility to keep an eye them as they may be led out of their depth by your children and find themselves in difficulties. You may not realise until too late that they are not comfortable in the water.

Kieran likes to travel with a fleet of little cars and vehicles, or various humanoid shapes with which he constructs wonderful games, these would nearly always attract an audience of young local children who were utterly entranced by these 'foreign' objects. At first they would just hang around watching but eventually they couldn't resist picking up the toys and joining in. When Kieran realised they weren't going to steal them and with encouragement from me he played happily with the children for ages, all language difficulties forgotten.

Culture

Everywhere you go people seem to like babies: people always want to cuddle a baby and a foreign baby is especially interesting. There are some cultural differences in child rearing and it pays to have a rudimentary knowledge of what they are. In many Asian countries babies are simply not allowed to cry for long; someone will always pick them up the moment they draw breath to yell. This should be borne in mind when yours decides to let you know that all is not well with their world. You will be expected to do something; it is not good enough to protest that they will soon drop off to sleep and are only crying because they are tired. Babies are to be rocked, cuddled, carried and soothed immediately they show signs of distress, and you will get dirty looks and quite possibly a graphic illustration from an indignant grandmother if your reactions are too slow!

In some cultures older children are also not expected to cry; this time you will be regarded as a weak parent if your children throw tantrums or scream their displeasure. If you find yourself losing your temper with your children, try not to shout or smack them if you have an audience. This may sound very hypocritical, but find some other way to (quietly) defuse the situation. Asians in particular don't seem to chastise their children very much, at least in public, and they may be shocked to find you do.

Why Asian children are, in general, so well behaved and mature without any overt signs of strong discipline is a mystery to me. As babies they are coddled, taken everywhere, fed on demand, always carried and tended to by one or another of an often large extended family. They sleep with their parents and are rarely excluded from any family happening. They do not have set routines, but sleep when tired and eat when hungry.

From the moment they are walking and talking they are expected to be capable of helping out with family chores and are given increasing responsibility. By age five they may be preparing family meals over open fires using vicious looking cleavers, looking after babies or relieving their parents in the family shop. The boys may be cutting crops with large machetes from age three, without a noticeable increase in limbless people in the population. They are taught, quite firmly, what is expected from them in their society and seem to take their place in that society with amazing maturity at a very early age. They are treated as small adults and are expected to behave as such. This doesn't stop them from having fun and playing games with all the gusto associated with childhood, but only when with other children, with adults they behave as expected. Despite having tried to incorporate many of the above child rearing techniques in raising my own children, I have not managed to achieve this state with them!

Culture Shock
You may find that your normally outgoing, assertive two-year old becomes very dependent and 'clingy' when you first start travelling. This is normal. When everything familiar has disappeared, what else can they do but hang on to what remains? Don't try to make them 'snap out of it', don't try and force them to make friends with strangers or get them to stay with the lovely lady who runs your hotel and is longing for the chance to look after them, you will only make matters worse. Try to be extra comforting, take them with you wherever you go, tell them where you are going and what you hope to see there. Let them know that everything is perfectly normal and fine, and just give them a bit of extra coddling.

Generally it doesn't take too long for children to regain their sense of security, if handled with understanding.

This 'understanding' may not come easily, especially at the beginning of a trip. If you are also feeling disoriented and a bit uncertain of what you are doing, and if it is your first trip beyond a familiar western environment you may be feeling a little insecure yourself. Try not to let your child sense this. Stay close to the hotel, make short walking trips in 'your neighbourhood', eat at the hotel if you feel more comfortable there, and only set off on excursions when you feel ready to handle it.

As a parent you are, of course, expected to know everything – you are the source of all wisdom and strength. No matter how vulnerable you are feeling, now is not the time to disillusion your child. Be decisive, even if you are not sure what it is you are deciding. If you need to find out something ask questions from anyone you meet who is likely to have the information you require. Other travellers you meet in restaurants or on the street are good sources of information regarding places to eat, ways of getting to places, where to change money, etc, and they are usually happy to pass on what they have learned.

At some stage your children, depending on their age, may become upset by the poverty and suffering they see in some countries. Trying to avoid it, or pretending it isn't there, or it isn't so bad, or suggesting that somehow these people are different and don't feel things the same way, is doing your children a disservice and denying them the opportunity to use their travelling experience to its fullest extent. Of course, that doesn't mean that you should launch into a full political and ideological treatise on the Third World, it is generally enough to answer only those questions the children will ask, namely 'why'.

Try to instil in your children respect for the people they are meeting. This means that besides insisting that the standards you would normally set are maintained, you must try yourself not to give way to expressions of disdain when you are talking to your partner or other travellers about the local people. This is something you always think you don't do, but how often has some local frustration caused you to lose your temper or talk about 'these people' in tones of less than affection? Having your children with you may not prevent such occasions arising, but try to be aware how you speak about and to the people you meet. Remember that your children are still using you as their role model, even more so now that their world is so totally different and their usual guidelines are gone.

The fact that 'grown-up' people don't understand English may cause your children some hilarity; they may feel very superior when they use the wrong word or talk 'like babies'. It's a good opportunity to introduce them to the language of the country by teaching them a few basic words – 'hello', 'goodbye', 'please', and 'thank you' are good starting points – and firmly squash such incipient chauvinism by asking them how much of the local language they can speak!

Babysitters

Babysitters are a possibility in many countries. Large hotels in tourist areas can often make babysitting arrangements but it's much nicer when the little local hotel in which you are staying is run by a family, and the daughters would just love to look after your children. You can come to some arrangement as to when and how much; usually it will be a very small financial cost. If you are planning a long stay in one place, you can often organise someone to look after the children. Enquire at your hotel, or if you know someone in the area ask them to check it out for you.

In general even young children (by our standards) will be very competent baby minders. Most young girls have been trained by looking after their younger siblings. Children as young as five often have total responsibility for little babies while their parents work.

While I don't suggest you hire a five-year-old, from 11 years upwards you will have a competent 'nanny'. In Asia in particular I really don't feel you have to be as cautious or wary with strangers as you would in most western countries. Obviously there is always some uneasiness with people you don't know, but certainly in the villages and smaller places your child should be perfectly safe with a local 'caretaker'. Leave snacks and drinks, and for the first few times at least try to be gone for only a short time and tell the babysitter when you will be back. If you have any instructions make sure they are understood – get an interpreter if necessary.

With very small children it doesn't really matter whether the babysitter speaks English – 'no' is fairly clear in most languages – but with older children it will help if the babysitter speaks even a little English. Tashi and Kieran have enjoyed a wide variety of babysitters and are quite happy to sit and draw with those who don't speak English very well or at all. The three of them use pictures to communicate, drawing houses, animals and so on and giving the names of things they draw in both languages. I've found the babysitters have enjoyed this as much as the children.

Money

More is best – it has long been recognised that two cannot live as cheaply as one and you soon realise that taking the kids is not as easy or as cheap as it may have seemed when the child in question was theoretical rather than actual. You can still travel cheaply with children, and in many places cheaper hotels can be more fun with children and for children than the multi-storey, western-style, 'behave yourself, people are watching' type.

If, however, you are travelling on a shoestring you need to be prepared to upgrade how you travel and where you eat. Concrete floors may be fine, but if you have a child who is crawling you may suddenly realise that the concrete floor, besides being hard, is not always that clean. Or if your child is toddling, shakily, and there is no lock on the toilet door, and the toilet is just a hole in the floor, the stress of watching every moment may not be worth the money you're saving.

Other hassles of very cheap hotels may be the impossibility of keeping out mosquitoes. The rooms may be poorly soundproofed and every noise is audible, including your child lustily bellowing for a drink at 2 am. The bathroom may not have a bath or shower or sink, so washing your children may be a little difficult. Somehow cleanliness becomes more important when you are travelling with children.

Often what was acceptable to you alone is no longer so for your children. You may find that you feel more comfortable in more expensive hotels when you are travelling with children although you won't necessarily have to spend very much more to find places that are ideal for you and your children. You can still find places which are both comfortable and cheap in many countries in Asia, Africa and Latin America. We've stayed in superb places which were also very economical in places as diverse as Mexico, Indonesia, Kenya, Nepal and Peru.

Travelling with young children means that your days start early and usually end early when you have to feed them and get them to bed. So it's nice sometimes to stay in a flashier place which has little bungalows or rooms set around or near the dining area. You can feed the children early and get them to sleep and then go eat, taking turns to go back to the rooms, say, every 10 minutes to check that they are still asleep. It's nice to have an 'adult' meal occasionally.

Older children can usually stay up later and accompany you to dinner, but there are occasions when they are tired or you feel like having a more adult dinner. If the restaurant is in the hotel or very close and it's a small hotel you could leave the children drawing or reading and ask somebody at the hotel to keep an eye on them and call you if necessary. Write down where you will be and make sure your children know exactly where you are.

With small children in particular long bus or train trips are unlikely to be much fun. Being willing to spend more money is useful for those occasions when a flight will get you from A to B in a tenth of the time. Look for easy ways out; in many countries there are long distance taxis which can cut hours off a trip, will stop when you want and aren't so crowded – all great advantages when travelling with children. Travelling at a slower pace, staying longer in one place or breaking up a longer trip into separate sections are all ways of breaking the monotony for kids. Upgrading your eating places is also a good idea. In many places you will find local eating stalls or restaurants that are safe, appetising and cheap but there will also be times when all that is available is an expensive hotel or restaurant, either because other places look too unsavoury, what is on offer simply doesn't appeal to young tastes or because there is simply nothing else. While you may be prepared to eat what is available, snack on fruit or nuts or even just go without a meal, your child may not.

Apart from the health or convenience situation, there will definitely be times when all your children want are a hamburger, French fries and a cold milkshake. Most big hotels can provide a suitable facsimile almost anywhere in the world and the indulgence is probably worthwhile for the pleasure it will bring. It also helps children to feel that not everything has been left behind. Children have no real concept of time, so a few weeks is a very long time. To tell your children to wait until they get home in a few weeks for familiar food, is like saying in January that 'next Christmas you'll get to decorate the tree'. Children can feel that they are never going to see home or anything familiar again. The kind of meal that they recognise can help them feel a little more secure, and also reassure them that they won't have to eat 'strange food' for ever.

Room service should not be despised either. Having dinner in your room when you are all tired and can't face the hassle of going to a restaurant is cheap at the price. Likewise a leisurely breakfast in your room after a week spent getting up and dashing out and off to see and do, is also a luxury worth having.

Involve Them
While you are travelling, keep your children informed of what your plans are. Tell them where you are going, what you want to see, how you will get there – all the details. Not only will your children find this interesting but it also helps to give them a sense of security. Help them choose postcards to send back, even if you do the writing. Let them have some local money and encourage them to make transactions at the market (with you overseeing of course). In countries like India and Nepal, markets have stall after stall selling brightly coloured, plastic bangles, necklaces and wonderful

hair ornaments which will totally delight most little girls. Buy some for their friends back home.

In Africa Kieran became hooked on the concept of bargaining and would wander through the markets trying to unload unwanted possessions for a much more interesting carving; the stall holders were usually so tickled at his cheek that he never came away empty handed! Once on a bus he entertained a large group of hawkers with his sales pitch in a desperate attempt to own a Masai shield!

When walking through the streets of Cuzco in Peru we were often taken aback at how much Tashi noticed for herself, and also how much we found to talk with her about what we were seeing. Statues are interesting; if not intrinsically, they can make great climbing frames (except for Buddha statues, *never* climb on Buddha statues). Even temples and buildings can be made to seem interesting if you have a little bit of knowledge of their history or architecture. Don't assume that some things are not interesting to your children because of their age. You may be surprised; your children will be interested in almost everything – given the chance. But keep it all in moderation; if you march them around while you spout information and act like a school teacher on a 'cultural' trip you may well just turn them off.

This all means that you have to be prepared yourself. You don't have to know everything – dates and architectural styles are probably not what children are interested in – but there are so many 'things' which have a story or legend behind them. Take the time and trouble to learn a bit about it, to understand why people are doing what they are doing. If your children ask and you don't know, find out – look up your books or ask someone. You will be surprised how interesting this will be for you as well as your children.

Travellers' Tales

AUSTRALIA & THE PACIFIC

THE AUSTRALIAN OUTBACK

Travelling round Australia, our home country, hardly qualifies for language difficulties, coping with the Third World or making do with strange food. But our Australian travels have included a number of terrific outback trips, all of them so much fun that we're already planning the next ones. At a glance this would seem surprising – it certainly surprised us – because outback travel in Australia is essentially long, often with lonely and tedious road trips (hardly inspiring stuff for travel with kids). In actual fact the hours on the road have indeed been rather tedious at times but the compensations at the end of the day and the interesting breaks you can often organise along the way more than make up for it.

All our outback trips have been fairly short ones; just a couple of weeks slotted in during Tashi and Kieran's shorter school vacations. Our first outback trip was a circuitous route from Melbourne down to Adelaide, finishing at the Australian Grand Prix (in the Australian jargon I'm a bit of a petrol head).

Our first destination was Broken Hill, an outback mining town, where we wandered the old town and visited the town's curious art galleries. We explored Silvertown, the nearby ghost town which featured in the film *Mad Max* and we saw kangaroos, emus and camels.

Then we continued down the road and turned off the bitumen to follow the long unsealed road which skirts round the edge of Lake Eyre and crosses the dingo-proof fence – a sure sign that you're in the outback – before arriving at Arkaroola. This is a sort of Australian dude ranch; a place where you can feel like you've come to grips with the outback but the air-conditioning and cold beer is still close to hand. This certainly doesn't stop it from being a lot of fun; there's magnificent scenery and lots of wildlife to be seen and the heart-stopping 4WD ridge-top ride to be experienced.

From Arkaroola we travelled south through the superb scenery of the Flinders Ranges to Wilpena Pound, one of Australia's natural wonders. This immense natural bowl looks like a fantastically large meteorite crater and has some wonderful bushwalks, some of them quite short enough for small children, and lots of wildlife to be seen. Interspersed with these longer stops we did some shorter walks, had meals in

country pubs populated by laconic outback Australians, and spent the odd night here and there. Altogether it hardly seemed possible that we'd covered as many miles as we did.

The next trip we drove all the way from Melbourne to Alice Springs, more or less in the dead centre of Australia. Again there were some long hauls on the way up to Ayers Rock but various stops along the way and a couple of days in the eerie outback opal mining town of Coober Pedy (yes they filmed another of the *Mad Max* sagas here too) cut the tedium. Ayers Rock is one of Australia's major tourist attractions – probably *the* major outback attraction – but the day or two most visitors spend here is far too short to really appreciate it. There is all sorts to be seen and done, from dawn walks with the rangers to climbing the rock itself. 'I've climbed Ayers Rock' is a standard Australian claim which Kieran could notch up at four years of age.

From Ayers Rock we headed to Kings Canyon, a miniature Grand Canyon, another of Australia's finest natural features and the site for some superb walks and views. We spent a night at the Wallarra Ranch road house, where everybody was sat down to dinner and served together and where, according to the books, I must have set my daughter on the path to a misspent youth by shooting pool with her in the bar after-wards. A few days in and around Alice Springs followed, along with a stay at the Ross River Homestead, another chance to try outback life, camel rides and a good base for the gorges and ghost towns this side of Alice. This central Australian trip ended with the quick and easy route back south. We loaded the car on the Ghan train one afternoon; 24 hours later we were back in Adelaide and then we drove back overnight to Melbourne, the kids sleeping the whole way.

Both these outback trips had covered a pretty fair selection of rough and ready outback roads but they'd all been done in our regular take-the-kids-to-school Mazda; there's no need for 4WD and fancy equipment on trips like that.

Outback trip three was a longer one around the coast of Western Australia from Darwin to Perth. In fact this one really was a bit too long; in retrospect we should have kept the kids out of school for a week as the balance between good times and long hours driving was tilted a little too much towards the long hours. There was plenty more we could have done, given time, and another week would have made it a rather more relaxed trip.

Which isn't to say we didn't do and see plenty; there were crocodiles, river trips in the Katherine Gorge and more crocodiles up in the north of the Northern Territory. There were walks at Kununurra and Halls Creek, the prison boab tree (hollow trees you can climb inside are sure fire children pleasers) at Derby, and at Broome we saw Walt Disney's *101 Dalmatians* in an open-air cinema which you walked into rather than drove. We lazed on beaches, body surfed in the Indian Ocean, talked to the dolphins at Monkey Mia (they swim right up to you in the shallow water) and crowned the whole trip with overnight stays with friends in Perth and Adelaide.

Car trips are a standard part of many vacations and they can be horror stories if they don't go well. Our kids are no more enthusiastic about being cooped up in a car than any others but we seem to have mastered the art of covering long distances relatively painlessly. Lots of in-car entertainment is one answer; tape cassettes they can listen to, paper and pens for drawing on knee tables, and games to play. Interesting stops are another; if you can get out and do something or take a short walk for half an hour it makes all the difference. The short stops break up the day's driving while longer stops will break up the whole trip. It's amazing how a really interesting and active day spent doing things totally wipes out all memory of the previous day spent driving. Knocking off a good chunk of distance when the kids are asleep also helps. Our standard technique is to make the first leg after school on Friday; we depart straight from school, stop at some country pub for dinner, bed the kids down after that and drive till around midnight. When you finally stop you've covered pretty much a whole day's driving and the kids haven't even noticed!

Tony Wheeler

NEW ZEALAND

Our first trip to New Zealand was years back, well before we had children, on a motorcycle. I've subsequently returned on several occasions by myself but the next time Maureen and I went there together was with the children in early '87 when Tashi was six and Kieran was four. We only travelled in the South Island where we did a more-or-less complete circuit in a campervan.

It was our first experience of campervan travelling and we found it quite fun, although the weather was often decidedly cool as autumn faded towards winter. One of the unexpected pleasures of campervan travel was hitch-hikers! Lots of young backpackers stand by the roadside with their thumbs out in New Zealand and with a hefty campervan we had enough room to operate a real bus service. Leaving Wanaka one morning we picked up every hitch-hiker strung out along the road from town. For the kids it was a good international education as we picked up 11 different nationalities during our circuit, and for us we knew the kids always had someone in the back to talk and play with! There was one particular young Englishman whom we picked up three times during our South Island circuit.

Some of the New Zealand highlights, from the children's point of view, included being stranded in a veritable sea of sheep down one back country road and seeing a superb display of sheep corralling by an expert sheep dog near Queenstown. At the campsite near the Fox Glacier one late afternoon we watched two keas, the large and playful New Zealand alpine parrots, moving purposefully through the site, knocking over every single garbage bin in order to inspect the contents! Wanaka proved a hit with a wonderful Brontosaurus slide in the lakeside children's park and a helicopter trip up on to the Fox Glacier was another high spot.

New Zealand's campsites are almost always very well

equipped and although the campervan was set up for cooking we did occasionally use the campsite's kitchen facilities.
Tony Wheeler

COOK ISLANDS

Pacific Islands are great places to simply relax and do very little. We visited the Cook Islands in 1986 when Tashi was five and Kieran was three. A single road curves around the main island of Rarotonga, bordering long stretches of beautiful, palm fringed beaches. There is great swimming and snorkelling in shallow, warm, blue water and plenty of 'island nights' where the traditional dancing is done with verve and grace. The children loved the 'hula' dancing and on one great night in Aitutaki we were festooned with flowers and watched not only the beautiful local girls swaying to the island music but a few decidedly un-lithe grandmothers shaking their bulk with great gusto as they sashayed to and from the bar.

The people are as friendly as they are claimed to be and there are many surprisingly good restaurants in Avarua, the main town on Rarotonga. The accommodation is mainly motel-style, generally with self-catering facilities, so Tony and I would often feed the children and then go off to enjoy an evening out, leaving the kids with a local babysitter. The hotels had telephone numbers of babysitters to ring, and we were delighted with the girl who looked after our children – not only was she quite happy to read to the children and draw with them but she also taught them to dance!

The trip included one frightening interlude, at Aitutaki, when a party of us planned a fishing trip to be followed by a beach barbecue at an island in the lagoon. On our way out a sudden storm blew up; we could barely see due to the heavy rain and since the lagoon is dotted with coral heads there was a real danger of hitting something. We dropped anchor and pitched around for a while and it was not reassuring to find there were not enough life jackets to go around. Swimming for it with two small children was not part of our plans! Fortunately the storm gradually abated and as we were all soaked and a little miserable the general vote was not to carry on. Our skipper had managed to spear a number of fish so we eventually had the barbecue behind his house, back on the main island!

Occasionally on our trips I wonder if travel is always so beneficial for the children; there are some tastes they acquire which are of dubious value – like both my children's predilection for the hotel bars! Once we were staying on the beach just outside Avarua where the hotel consisted of bungalows amongst the palm trees and a little open-air bar right on the beach. The water was very shallow and the beach private so I was quite happy to let the children run wild. One afternoon I hadn't seen them for a while, but supposed they were on the beach. I was on my own with the children for a few days so I decided to go to the bar for a cold drink and maybe find some adults to chat to. At the bar there were a few New Zealanders, and two small bartenders! Kieran popped up behind the bar and asked me what I wanted; Tashi, under the supervision of the waitress, put my drink together with considerable aplomb and professionalism, right down to the little umbrella! I tried pretending I didn't know them!

Maureen Wheeler

Getting There & Around

FLYING

There's more than a hint of truth in that saying about there being just two classes of travel – 1st class and with children. Flying with children can definitely be an endurance test.

I always loved flying: I would get a window seat, a few magazines or books, headset, movie, food, a few glasses of wine – bliss. To me the excitement of going places is all connected with airports and planes. Children changed all that.

With babies flying is generally more difficult than with older children simply because you have to work so hard to keep them happy – nursing them, playing with them, singing to them. And if you don't keep them happy they cry, and then see how friendly your neighbours are! Add to this the strain of changing nappies in the cramped toilets and the difficulties of eating your meal with a baby on your knee and you may decide to stay home!

Toddlers are also hard-going as travel companions; a long air trip can be pure torture for an 18 month to three year old, not to mention the parents. Whilst a baby may be kept happy by your proximity and undivided attention, herculean efforts are required to amuse and distract toddlers; books, toys and snacks can only go so far, usually not more than a few hours. Hopefully all their misspent energy will result in a long sleep, but don't count on it!

From three years on it does get easier (doesn't everything?) The children can amuse themselves for a while with drawing and simple games. They can invent imagination games with a few well chosen toys, the headphones tuned to the childrens' channel will keep them amused for a while, even the movie will put in a little time. They can feed themselves, with supervision, from their tray and the novelty of being offered drinks will usually keep them in a good humour. It is also easier to persuade them to lie down and have a sleep. With one child aged eight and one six, we find flying has regained some of its previous enjoyment. Sometimes we even manage to get two window seats and for shorter flights (or shorter periods of time on longer flights) the two children can sit together. Occasionally one of us has to replace one of them to restore peace and amity, but in general it works well.

Fares & Baggage Allowance

Children under two, provided they are accompanied by a fare-paying adult, pay 10% on international flights. Only one 10% fare is allowed per adult, any other children have to pay the children's fare. Children on 10% fares do not get a seat (they're expected to sit on your lap if necessary) or any baggage allowance. Nor do they get a meal; you're supposed to bring food for them or let them pick off your tray.

In practice, however, some allowance will be made. Airlines usually make an effort to ensure that if the flight is less than full, passengers with small children are given the benefit of spare seats. Similarly, necessary items for the baby during the flight can be brought on as cabin luggage. 'Necessary items' can be loosely interpreted, although it generally means food, nappies and clothes. Most (but not all) airlines will allow a pusher/stroller to be carried onto the plane. And it's very rare that there isn't a spare meal or two left over at meal times. Although you cannot, officially at least, bring a baby's carrycot on board the airlines will usually carry it free. They ask that it be collapsible if possible, but as long as it doesn't exceed 76 by 40 by 30 cm that's OK. They don't specify what it can weigh but as long as it's not over about 10 kg you should have no problems.

Children's fares in relation to adult's fares vary to some extent. In general it seems that children are classified as from two to 12 years of age for international flights, and three to 12 years of age for domestic flights. Children usually pay 50% of the adult fare but on discount fares it is often 67%, and these days a high proportion of the regular fares are classified as discount fares. The age is at the time of departure, if your child passes the critical age while

you're away that's no problem. Once your child has turned 12 all the discounts end, they're full fare payers from then on.

Children do get the full baggage allowance and if you're traveling somewhere tropical, where your clothes and baggage requirements are lightweight, you may find yourself with lots of spare baggage allowance. This can be very useful if you wish to bring back a large piece of local exotica. On a couple of occasions we've managed to come back from Bali with quite large stone carvings as part of our luggage. Coming back from Mexico, where the baggage allowance is by the piece rather than by weight, four of us times two pieces would have given us enough room to start a small Mexican crafts shop!

Sometimes in Asia the regulations have to be played around with, for reasons other than economics. Once in Nepal we were trying to get on a flight from Pokhara back to Kathmandu. We were told there were not enough seats – unless Tashi was under two? 'Yes', we said, with very straight faces, even though Tashi was only days away from being three, several sizes larger than the average Nepalese two year old and very obviously not a toddler.

Service

Airlines and airports offer quite a range of services and in general are very sympathetic to travelling parents' and their children's needs. Some airlines really are better than others at catering for children, some give the distinct impression that the flight at- tendants' training is much more heavily inclined towards pouring the wine properly rather than coping with toddlers.

It's quite easy to see the airlines that do think about children and their parents and often a little thought is much more appreciated than all the free colouring books:

Pre-boarding small children and their parents. You start the trip on the wrong foot if you have to queue for ages getting to your seat, fighting your way down a crowded aisle with your carry-ons, your children's carry-ons and (if it's an odd-hours departure) quite possibly sleepy or bad tempered children as well.

Supplying childrens' meals on request. Most airline food is unsuitable for children – it just doesn't accord with their tastes. Some American airlines will provide chicken and chips or sausages and chips which are much more appetising for most children, however, it does not seem to be standard practice for many airlines.

Serving children's meals separately. It takes very little effort for the flight attendants to bring all the small children their meals before they start the general meal service. That way your child can have got their meal out of the way before yours even arrives, and you're not stuck with trying to cope with two precariously balanced meals at once.

Simply treating children as real human beings. On vacation time flights I always appreciate the captain who prefaces announcements with 'ladies and gentlemen, boys and girls'. Older children love flight deck visits which some airlines manage to put on during the flight and a good children's channel on the entertainment system can be a real life saver on long flights. Some airlines even have activities books which tie in with the children's channel.

At the end of the day, however, no amount of cheerful, competent, well thought out service can match lots of empty seats around you.

The least crowded flights are often the very best ones as far as flying with children is concerned. With a couple of seats to stretch over small children can sleep just as comfortably as they do at home. A good flight route can make a real difference as well; children dislike being woken up in the middle of the night in order to stand around in some God-forsaken airport terminal even more than adults do.

All airlines carry bassinets on their long distance flights, but they are only useful for very young children. Pillows and blankets are also available.

Special diets, such as non-salted, low cholesterol, vegetarian, kosher, etc, should be booked at least 48 hours in advance. If you require snacks rather than full meals for your child or yourself, you can book this with the airline. You can also order baby food, or bring it yourself and they will heat it up.

The only problem with leaving everything to the airlines is that you may not always be able to get what you want when you need it. For instance, your plane is leaving just at the time your children are usually going to bed, and you may have to leave home mid-afternoon. The ideal time to feed your children is probably when you are sitting in the departure lounge. If you have some sand-wiches, fruit or a yoghurt you can have a picnic dinner there and then, or you could buy them a meal at the airport. Otherwise by the time you're up and flying, the pre-dinner drinks have been served and meal time finally rolls round it's going to be far beyond any possibility of a civilised meal!

Similarly, your children may be hungry before dinner arrives and the cabin crew are often busy preparing to serve dinner and may not be available to specially make up food. If you have something in your bag you can stop the demands before they become too vocal. I usually hang on to the crackers and cheese that come with airline dinners just in case they're needed at some other time.

One other important point. Arrive at the airport early and try to be among the first to check in. This is important if you are going to have any choice at all in the seat allocation, although airlines often will try to give families more choice than other passengers.

Airports

Most airports have a parents' room where you can change and feed your baby; some are excellent, others are inconvenient and dismal. There has been a swing towards making these facilities 'parents' rather than 'mothers' so these days fathers too can change and tend to their babies – no more excuses!

Few airports cater for older children at all, although there may be a few of the ubiquitous video games which are expensive and not much use to children under 10 years old. Singapore's Changi Airport, which many of us rate the best in the world, actually has a wonderful play area for kids in the transit/departure area. There are even a series of science exhibits which children can manipulate and have fun with. Some other better airports are making similar 'user friendly' moves to cater for children.

What To Bring

There is a fine balance to be struck between bringing everything you can possibly think of that your child might need, and what you really do need for the flight.

For babies I bring something they can sleep on – a rug, a lambskin, or a 'cuddly'. See the Sleeping section for information on 'beds'. Bring enough nappies to last the journey; airlines do carry them but it is best to consider those as 'emergency supplies only'. Of course disposable nappies are the only kind to carry. For cleaning bring 'wet ones', a damp cloth in a plastic bag, lotion and cotton wool – whatever you like to use (I prefer the packaged wet baby wipes for convenience). A few bibs are a very good idea.

Plastic bin liners are good for storing dirty nappies, dirty clothes, wipes, etc, until you can dispose of them. Usually the crew will take them away, but you can't always expect them to be there right when you need them, and it is nicer to be handed a plastic bag containing a nasty object rather than the nasty object itself.

A waterproof change mat is useful. Although there is usually one toilet in each section which proclaims a fold down change table is within, I really have never found them to be very useful. How do you hold a wriggling child down on a flat, hard surface in a cramped aeroplane toilet and change a nappy at the same time? I find it easier to lay the mat on my seat and change the baby there, unless it is really too disgusting and likely to make me very unpopular with other passengers.

At least one change of clothing is necessary. Depending on the age of your baby, a few toys may also help. For children under six months they don't appear to be necessary; all the people around may provide enough interest. For children over six months toys that they can fiddle with seem to keep them occupied for a little while. Don't bring toys with lots of bits; you don't want to spend the flight picking up pieces from the floor. Don't bring too many toys either – a handful of tried and true favourites are all that is necessary.

I have been told that for small babies a plastic reclining infant seat – the type with the adjustable stand and handles at each side – is a useful item for carrying babies onto planes, and equally useful for feeding them in, and for getting them out of your arms for a while. I haven't tried it; it could be useful but it may also be a nuisance to carry around on your travels.

For children from 12 months up, you can start shedding some of the equipment. For long flights I would still bring something for sleeping on or with, and at least one change of clothes. For those out of nappies take at least a couple of pairs of pants; accidents happen even to 'trained' children when they are excited, or worse, have to wait in line too long for a vacant toilet. Wet wipes are still very useful, as is a general 'mopping up' cloth.

Toys and books are useful, but bear in mind the limitations. Pipe cleaners make unusual toys; they can be twisted into shapes and can make little people. Favourite dolls and teddies of course must be included, and coloured pencils and notepads to draw on. The cabin crew will hand out games, books, pencils, etc, when your children get on the plane. Thai International got top marks on one particular flight for a plastic bib which went on to cover many miles with Tashi and was really useful (Kieran got one on his 'maiden flight' also). They also gave out 'stickle bricks' to older children which is an excellent toy and passed many happy hours both on the plane and off. Many of the give-aways are pitched at an older age group but children are almost always pleased at getting things for free, and will always find something that can be used.

One very useful hint was passed on by my mother-in-law. Most children have a 'familiar' that must travel with them – a teddy, or a doll, or some such friend. To avoid having to carry this, and the baby, and the bags, tie elastic around its neck, so that there is a loop. This loop goes around your child's wrist. It means that even if you do have to carry 'friend', it can go around your wrist, or over the stroller handle, and still leave your hands free. This tactic prevents the nightmarish possibility that you may inadvertently leave it behind some place.

Other suggestions for coping with small children at airports include attaching a small but loud whistle to your childrens' jacket. Then if they get lost or even momentarily separated from you, they can give a good piercing blast. It gives them a sense of security also, although I suspect you will probably have to dissuade them from using it at inappropriate moments and hope they remember to use it at the appropriate one! Some people find toddlers' reins useful at the airport or other crowded places. I did try reins once or twice but it's a battle to get children to wear them and I didn't persevere.

As children get older the problems dwindle although on long flights they get bored, just as adults do. Adequate supplies of books, toys and games all help. Our children have made lots of intercontinental flights now and although they dislike being cooped up just as much as the next child they've never been any real problem.

Finally, planes are very dry, and this can make everyone feel uncomfortable. I like to take a spray can of Evian Mineral Water; the children usually think it is a lot of fun to spray it on their faces and it feels nice and fresh, and if you follow it with a little bland moisturising cream, it does take the tight, dry feeling away. A chap stick is also useful if you tend to get dry lips. Toothbrushes and toothpaste are good to have when you begin to feel unwashed and unkempt, and are also a good idea for the children, who invariably end up drinking more soft drinks and sweetened juice than you would normally allow.

If you find the dry air causes sore noses or sinus discomfort, try putting a scarf around their faces, like a bandit. Something made of light material, lightly placed across their noses may cause some localised humidity and ease the discomfort. I try to put the blanket lightly over their faces when they are asleep.

Food

If your baby takes a bottle, then bring the bottle and at least most of the food needed. Although airlines will provide baby food upon request, it is best to be self-sufficient; if there are more babies than expected on the flight supplies of nappies and food can be quickly depleted. Also you may get held up somewhere unexpectedly and your supplies may have to go further than planned, so take what you calculate you need and perhaps a bit more. For quick, easy feeding on planes and in airports, bring jars of baby food, rather than cans. Two spoons (one for you to feed them with, one for them to feed themselves) and a plastic dish are also a good idea, although you can feed straight from the jar.

In many Third World countries domestic flights don't operate to the same standards as international services. It may be a good idea not to ask the crew to wash your bottles or make up formula. Try to bring enough clean bottles to last the journey. Although the water is generally purified, it is best to be on the safe side. It's not uncommon to see signs on aircraft water supplies warning you that you should not drink the water other than from the water fountains.

If your baby is breast fed, bring some juice and a bottle. Babies need to drink quite a lot in planes, and nursing mothers may find they seem to be continuously feeding their child. Frequent drinks of juice and water are a good idea to give the mother a break. The little bottles of juice for babies which are designed to take a standard feeding nipple are a good idea. They are sealed until you need them, you just take off the top and replace it with a nipple and usually there is just the right amount there. You don't have to worry about leakages, or juice spoiling.

Everyone gets dehydrated on planes, so nursing mothers have to be especially careful to increase their fluid intake (not alcohol though). Use the water fountains frequently or drink mineral water.

Airline meals are generally very much inclined towards adult tastes and often children will do no more than pick at them. Check when you book your ticket if they will supply a snack or child's meal. Juice is freely available, as are soft drinks, but if you prefer not to give your child juice with sugar or preservatives you will have to bring it with you. The small bottles of baby juice are very conveniently sized even for older children, and are sugarless and without preservatives.

One very important item for this age group is a trainer cup (one with a spout). These were so useful I always packed two, just in case one got lost along the way. Drinking juice or anything out of plastic cups is quite a difficult feat for small children; it invariably ends up on you, them, your seat or, if you're lucky, the floor. If you just make a blanket rule that while on the plane all drinks must be drunk from the spout cup, your trip will be much drier.

If you do decide to bring snacks remember they will be spending quite a while in your bag; anything with a tendency to mush, crumble or sog is not a good idea. I'm afraid I leave my food principles behind when I fly with the children. I bring a large bag of sweets with which I bribe, cajole and cheer up when necessary.

Check list for babies:

lambskin, rug, cuddly
disposable nappies
change(s) of clothing/underpants
wet wipes, mopping up cloth
food, drinks
spoons, dish
bibs
bottle(s)
plastic bags
waterproof change mat
toys, books

Check list for older children:

trainer cup (cup with spout)
coloured pencils & notepads
games
books
Evian Spray
moisturising cream
chap stick
toothbrushes & toothpaste
change of clothes or top
plastic bags
wet wipes/cloth

Sleeping

All airlines carry bassinets on their long distance flights; but they
are only useful for very young children. Their dimensions are
between 58 and 70 cm long and about 30 cm wide, and about 20
cm deep. Pillows and blankets are available, although they are
usually only handed out on night flights. If you require a bassinet
you must ask for it in advance; it's a good idea to do this when you
book your ticket.

The bassinet either clips on to the bulkhead (the wall on which
the movie is shown) or hangs above your head on certain designated
seats in the window aisle. These are fine for very young babies, but
are really pretty small – if your baby is a normal to big size it can
be very cramped to lie in. They do, however, give you an area for
a baby to sit and play in.

Both my children slept on lambskins as babies, so I always
brought them on the plane with me. They are bulky, but can be
easily folded down into normal cabin luggage and it can be very
useful on long flights to have something familiar and comforting
for the child to sleep on. If your child has a favourite rug or blanket,
bring it with you if at all possible.

For older children it doesn't seem to matter; they will settle down
and sleep when they are ready, and the flight attendant will bring

blankets and cushions to make them comfortable. You can only hope for an extra seat to make life really easy!

Where to Sit

Where you sit can be quite important. Parents with small children are generally placed in the first row of seats facing the bulkhead, on the theory that there is more leg room. Well there may be, but on many aircraft the bulkhead seat row has fixed armrests which the tables fold down into, which means that if you are lucky enough to score a vacant seat beside you, your child can't lie out flat because the armrest won't budge. Even if there is no vacant seat, if the armrest won't lift you can't spread your child across their seat and your knee.

The extra leg room can, however, be used to make a bed on the floor. The crew will supply you with pillows and blankets and if you can persuade your child to lie down on it, a toddler-size person could be quite comfortable. Airlines don't permit you to sleep on the floor, however, except for take-off and landing or if there is turbulence the crew will generally turn a blind eye to where small children end up.

I usually avoid the bulkhead because when the movie is on you are right beneath it and a child who won't sleep is harder to persuade when the flickering images are right above. It also means that if you stand up, which you seem to have to do a lot with children, you are in everyone's way. It is also less easy to turn your light on for all those emergencies for which you need illumination, as this affects the picture for everyone behind. Another hassle is that any other parents with babies will be right there with you. Who needs someone else's problems? If your children don't usually cry, sitting beside someone with children who do cry might just set them off.

If it is to be a long flight I try to ask for seats in the middle section, between the two aisles, on the theory that there are more seats in that section than between the aisle and the window, so you have more chance of being able to stretch out if there are vacant seats. The cabin crew are generally very helpful and understanding and will try to find you extra seats if at all possible. Also if you and your family have three seats in a row of four and an individual stranger sits down in the vacant seat left, one look at your contingent is usually enough to send them looking for alternative seating, so you may still wind up with an extra seat. If you have two adults and two or more children you can always go on a scouting trip through the plane; you may find that by splitting up you can get very comfortably organised.

Medication

Sedating children for flights is a tricky question. I don't like to use any medication unless absolutely necessary, but when the children were smaller I found that no matter how tired they were they could keep themselves awake through sheer excitement, and once they got beyond a certain point they were miserable, cranky and exhausted, but still not asleep. Some children simply sleep when they are tired, but not all. On the occasions that I did use sedatives I found them very helpful; the children arrived in much better shape to cope with the first few days in a new place, and we had not had a fraught flight.

Another consideration is that, if you have spent too many hours awake with your children you will also be pretty exhausted and unable to deal with them with the patience necessary to help them to settle in. Your doctor can probably advise you on what to give them. I used Phenergan (Promethazine), an antihistamine which is useful for travelling as it can help combat travel sickness. A 10 mg tablet worked fine for Kieran age 18 months, but it took 25 mg for four year old Tashi. The tablets are small enough for very young children and can be given in a spoonful of jelly or whatever. The alternative of 25 ml of Phenergan liquid is much more difficult to get down them.

You must give them the sedative before they reach the totally miserable stage as it may be too late to have much effect later.

Now that the children are older I don't find it necessary to use anything to help them sleep and even if they don't sleep on shorter flights neither makes a fuss or causes problems for anyone else.

Preparation for the Flight

It is a good idea to plan for a calm, relaxed day for the 24 hours before your flight. Eat small, bland meals (nothing too taxing for the digestive system), go to bed early and try to stop children from becoming too excited. How? I don't really know, but avoid last-minute hassles, rows about who put what where, and who is the idiot who did such and such. Get to the airport in time to organise everything and everyone calmly. Walk around and look at the shops, the planes; talk quietly about going on the plane, and what it will be like. Try to keep everything as relaxed as possible.

Motion Sickness

Travel sickness is something which affects lots of children. The only time our children have been very sick when flying was on a short but extremely bumpy domestic flight in Australia. And by a stroke of luck we checked in rather late and had to sit three and one; luck of the toss I got the one seat left in business class while Tony sat with the kids back in steerage! Along with half of the other passengers on this flight Tashi and Kieran were both airsick! We've also had one bout of seasickness with them, in this case on an equally bumpy high speed catamaran trip out to the Great Barrier Reef. Under more normal circumstances, touch wood, neither is prone to motion sickness.

If your children are prone to motion sickness, it's probably best to have something to hand just in case. There are certainly some trips which would test anyone's stomach muscles – Great Barrier Reef trips in Australia can be notoriously bumpy, flights in light aircraft over mountains can have you soaring up and down like a yo-yo and there are some equally stomach stirring bus trips in the Third World. Ginger is an old fashioned remedy for travel sickness which is becoming fashionable again. You can buy ginger capsules from many health food stores. It is best to use the capsules because fresh ginger, in the amounts you would require to take, could burn the throat. Take one or two capsules about an hour before you are due to fly. The amount you require will probably be something you learn through experience. Check with the health food store you buy it from that the capsule dosage will be suitable for your child's age-group.

There are other preventative preparations available; again, ask your doctor. Note that some of these motion sickness medicines have the drawback that they can cause drowsiness. Also they must be taken before you start the trip; when you start to feel sick it's too late. If it's any consolation children seem to get over motion sickness remarkably quickly. On the reef trip already mentioned Kieran threw his breakfast violently over the side, and an hour or two later wolfed down the biggest lunch he'd ever eaten. And kept it down on the way back.

What to Wear on the Flight

Comfort is the main consideration. Regardless of where you're going or expected weather, cover all possibilities. You may be flying from winter to winter only to be delayed for hours en route at some height-of-the-hot-season hole with the airport air-conditioning out of operation and the temperatures soaring. You could just as likely end up shivering in a T-shirt in a freezing cold plane as it waits on the tarmac for caterers to settle a dispute. We flew from the plains of India to Moscow in the middle of winter once, and then spent an hour standing outside the aircraft while security searched for a missing bag. Fortunately we'd been trekking in Nepal and were well equipped with down jackets but some sari-clad women on the flight looked distinctly uncomfortable.

So regardless of what your destination is supposed to be, come prepared. A layer system of clothing works well. Track suits for children are a good idea, say a T-shirt, then track suit, and then a jumper or light parka.

For very young children the terry vest/undershirt and pants set of underwear is a good base; it looks fine if they want to strip down, and with a track suit on top you are prepared for anything. With babies a sleeveless body shirt, the kind that fastens over the nappy, is comfortable for climbing around in, keeps draughts out, and you can add a T-shirt if required. The all-in-one stretch sleep suits are good for babies when the temperature drops. A woollen cardigan or sweater with a hood completes the ensemble and covers all eventualities. If you want them to look cute when you arrive, you can carry their 'good wear' separately, but don't put it on too soon – when you are taxiing to the air bridge is time enough, as children can often foil their parents' best-laid plans.

For older children a track suit and T-shirt is a good idea and socks should always be worn if the flight is a long one as planes can get cold and feet really feel it!

Parents too should be comfortable; and if you are travelling with small children remember that it's possible to get spectacularly dirty by the time you arrive. Sticky finger prints, spilt food, regurgitated sweets, all have fewer places to go, so you will find yourself the main recipient. I usually wear stretch jeans, a dark sweat shirt and take a clean shirt to change into, again at the last moment. With older children, you can still be 'spilt on' and the considerations of comfort also apply.

Take-off (& Landing)

Young children are more sensitive to the air-pressure changes as you climb or descend. It is a good idea to hand out sweets or drinks at these times. Small babies will cry, which will clear their ears, but if you find this upsets you, giving them a drink will have the same effect. If your children have colds you should always check with the doctor before flying. Make sure there is no ear infection involved. He will probably advise a 'drying up' medication for the flight, and for small children who can't yet efficiently blow their noses a nasal spray may be recommended.

On a flight once in the States I had a bad cold and my ears wouldn't clear on descent. The pain was agonising and obviously it showed on my face, because the flight attendant (thank you) took one look at me, went away, and returned minutes later with two polystyrene cups. He had wadded paper napkins, soaked in hot water, into the bases of the cups. He suggested I put one over each ear. Feeling rather ridiculous, I did, and it worked! The hot air seemed to open up my blocked tubes and removed the pressure.

Changing Time Zones

Time changes can really disorient children. They will usually be tired anyway from the plane trip and with the alarm on their body clock going off at odd times they can become worn out and miserable (when they are not bouncing around in the early hours of the morning making you worn out and miserable). Although you may feel like just falling into bed when you reach your destination, if it is mid-morning on your new time try to keep going for the rest of the day. By all means take it easy; don't rush off sight-seeing for example. Relax and wind down, but try to make your bed time an appropriate one. The more quickly you can get on to the new time, the faster you will adjust. This doesn't mean that you have to keep your children awake come what may. They will probably nap anyway, but try to keep the going-to-bed rituals (bath, pyjamas, stories, etc) until the time that they will be actually going to bed.

If we arrive when it is early morning on the new time I would aim to have the children sleep before or around mid-day for an hour or two, then wake them up and keep them awake until a reasonable bed time. They will then hopefully sleep through the night and be on their way to adapting to the time change within a few days. If we arrive later in the day, I would try to keep them awake, but quiet until bedtime in the hope that they will sleep through the night

Again, sedatives are a possibility and may ensure that you all get a good nights' sleep for the first night. Once in New York, Tony and I spent a couple of nights playing with Tashi from 3 to 7 am, when she promptly went to sleep for a couple of hours, while we had to get up and get organised. We were staying with friends in a very small apartment so we couldn't just let her run wild, nor could we simply sleep on when everybody else was up. After a couple of days Tony and I were complete zombies and all I remember of New York on that occasion is vaguely wondering where I was and what I was doing there.

For the first three nights on a new time zone, if it is radically behind or ahead of your personal time clock, it may be worthwhile sedating the children. Being over-tired for the first few days of a trip can really get you all off to a bad start.

OTHER TRANSPORT
Long Distance

Making long trips by bus or train can be difficult with children when they've passed the tiny baby stage and not yet arrived at the able-to-amuse-themselves stage. Older children who are crawling or toddling usually hate having to sit still and in cramped buses or trains you don't have much room for movement. Quite often the buses lurch along in such a way that you really have to hang on to your children. If you do have to make a long trip, and there is no way you can break it up into smaller sections, all you can do is treat it like a plane trip. Make sure you have all you need readily available – drinks, snacks, books -whatever you think will work.

Throughout the Third World food and drink are sold by hawkers at stations, bus halts and on trains, but for very small children it's probably best to go prepared with all the food and drink you think they will need. The food available may not be suitable for your children, although you can often buy fruit or nuts, which are fine. In many places the meals on trains are pretty good, but it would still be good to have a supply of snacks that you know your child will like, and particularly a good supply of drinks.

Buses are often the most crowded and uncomfortable form of transport. You may have to hold your children for the entire journey, so if they are older than two it is probably worthwhile to pay for extra seats rather than to try and economise by keeping them on your knee. However, in many countries this is unlikely to work; there's no way your small children are going to stay on an extra seat, paid for or not, when many other people – old, pregnant or with children of their own – are standing. If you are travelling in a country or on a route where the buses are likely to be very crowded don't even bother getting extra seats for your children. Three people inevitably squeeze into a space intended for two anyway and you will be no exception.

In some Third World and developing countries the buses can be surprisingly luxurious – there may be videos, toilets and even meal service as you travel. Sometimes it can be a case of technological overkill – the air-conditioning may be turned to 'arctic' or the music may be turned up to just above the threshold of pain. Air-con buses in Malaysia have been described as 'meat lockers on wheels' they're so cold. And hour after hour of screeching Indian movies on buses on the sub-continent has to be some sort of inscrutable Asian torture.

In other parts of the Third World and on more remote routes the buses may be much more utilitarian. Remember the golden rule: if you are travelling with children, be prepared! Take all the food and drink you could possibly need. If you are travelling overnight then a blanket or warm clothes will help. In many places you will find the buses depart with quite amazing frequency so you rarely have to hang around for long. Bus trips can be a lot of fun, we've boarded local buses in Africa where we felt like we were the first white faces ever seen on that route and the welcome was a warm one.

For comfort, where there is a choice of bus or train, trains are probably a better bet. If the trip is a really long one, an overnight sleeper, if available, is always the best way to do it. Children love sleeping on trains, and small babies can at least lie down. Holding a small baby in your arms for a long period of time in hot weather is no fun for you or them.

If you do have to make a long trip, try to make sure that the next few days are spent somewhere nice and relaxing. Choose a comfortable hotel where the children can run around and enjoy themselves. Set up house for a few days, unpack the bags, frequent the same restaurants, give the children and yourselves as much time as you can manage to totally get the trip out of your system. While it may seem as though the children have forgotten all about the trip an hour after getting off the bus, the next time you reach the bus station you may find them yelling that they don't want to go. Never plan too many long journeys. Where they are unavoidable, space them as much as possible.

Older children will, of course, be bored on long bus trips, but they usually manage better for longer. Local people may talk to them, you can play all the usual 'travel games' and chatting about what you are seeing will all pass time. Have a treat for each hour after a certain period, even if it is only sweets or fruit, and take advantage of any stops. Always remember to make your children visit the toilet at every opportunity although kids are kids anywhere in the world and bus drivers always know what it means when you come striding up the aisle, child in hand. We've asked for unplanned pee stops all over the world!

In many Third World countries you can use taxis for long distance trips. These are always faster than buses and often not much more expensive. In Turkey they are known as *dolmus,* in the Middle East as service taxis. You also find them in some African countries, in Malaysia, and on some routes in Indonesia. Usually the principle is that they wait at a starting point (often near the bus station) until they have a full load, then off they go. Of course your family may well be a full load and often you can arrange to be taken right to your destination, not just dropped at the bus stop. Taxis may not have safety belts so be prepared to hang on to your children.

Rent-a-Cars

Rent-a-cars have spread far beyond the bounds of the western 'first world' in recent years and renting a car can make life much easier for the travelling family. We've rented cars in places as widespread as the Cook Islands, Mexico, Sri Lanka, Indonesia and Kenya. Renting cars in the Third World does have a number of special rules which don't usually apply at your local Avis, Budget or Hertz agency.

Where importing cars is difficult or expensive the cars may not be the latest models or in the best of mechanical condition. We've rented some decidedly tatty old Volkswagon Beetles over the years but as long as it keeps going who's complaining? Check it over carefully though. Is there a jack and wheelbrace for example? Have they noted that both the outside mirrors have been broken off (so you don't get billed for them later)? We could have saved ourselves a lot of trouble once in Sri Lanka if we'd insisted that some of the tyres were not going to last the distance.

Don't count on having safety belts or being able to get infant seats. Some countries are surprisingly up to the minute in this respect (wearing seat belts is compulsory in Singapore) but in others even if there were safety belts initially they're unlikely to be working. If you are planning to do a lot of travelling by car and you can work out a way of attaching it, you may think it worth bringing a child's safety seat with you. Once in Indonesia we met a surgeon from an American hospital casualty department who was, not unexpectedly, extremely cautious about car safety. He had brought metre upon metre of safety belt and his family literally tied themselves into their vehicle!

Don't count on the rate card. In the west there may be special weekend rates or longer period rentals. In the Third World you may simply have to bargain. In some places the rate is totally open to negotiation and they will ask whatever you look like you might pay. In others they'll be quite open about it, if you want a newer car you pay more, if you're willing to take a well worn example the rate will drop.

In some places it simply isn't worth renting a car. We rented a car once in Lima, Peru. It was fine for visiting places around the town but getting in and out of Lima was such a nightmare we wondered why we'd bothered. You can rent cars in Bangkok or Cairo but who on earth would bother? On the other hand we met a family once who rented a car in Japan – seemingly the last place on earth a foreigner would want to be saddled with driving themselves – but it had worked amazingly well. They had got to all sorts of remote villages where public transport was difficult and hence foreign visitors few and far between.

In some places renting cars is very easy and there is a wide choice of local operators and competitive rates – Mexico, parts of Indonesia, and Kenya are good examples. In others there may be a real car shortage and you'll only get one if you book well ahead. Read up on the situation where you're going.

You don't need to drive yourself. The cost of renting a car is often far higher than hiring a chauffeur in the Third World and in some places, like India, you simply can't rent cars to drive yourself but can easily get a car with driver.

Local Transport

Within cities, towns and villages there is a wide choice of transport – depending on where you're going you may come across buses, taxis, auto-rickshaws, horse carriages, bicycle-rickshaws or end up walking! In Asia children usually love bicycle-rickshaws. They're a good, cheap way to get around and rickshaw wallahs usually like children – after all they're easier to pedal around than adults! Auto-rickshaws are small three-wheeler devices powered by motorcycle engines. You find them in parts of Indonesia, on the sub-continent and in Thailand, where they are known as *samlors*, Thai for 'three wheels'. Indonesian *bemos* and *colts*, Papua New Guinean PMVs, Thai *songthaews*, East African *matatus* are all other forms of transport you may come across.

Bicycles

In many places in Asia, particularly on the sub-continent or in China, bicycles are easily available in touristed areas and are a good, fun way to get around. Unfortunately you won't often find

child seats available, but if you're staying some place for awhile you could get one made. We stayed in Kathmandu for awhile once, sought out the cane furniture making area and had cane bicycle seats made up, which we tied on to the rear carriers of our rented bikes. We managed to sell them to other travelling parents when we left.

Strollers & Backpacks

A folding, reclining stroller

can be a lifesaver. We took one on our first long trip with Kieran when we went to Indonesia. At four months he was too young for a backpack carrier but by that time he was too heavy for the front packs. Taking the stroller was easy enough and it was very useful. Obviously, a stroller is no good at all if you plan to go trekking on mountain paths, isolated tracks or beaches. It is strictly useful for day-to-day excursions to the restaurant, shops, hotels and around towns.

The Indonesians thought it was the most amazing idea; their babies are carried by one or other of the many relatives and neighbours who are always within arm's reach. When there are only two sets of arms available, one set generally occupied with a bag full of important items to travellers, and perhaps with another child to contend with, some mechanical means of transport has to be found. The stroller was also great in restaurants; it meant that I could strap Kieran in an upright position and eat my meal without having to keep him on my knee – a risky situation – and he was generally content to sit and look around. Because it reclined he could, while he was young, sleep in it so we didn't have to rush back to the hotel when he started hinting it was time for his nap.

Backpacks are good for children who can sit up by themselves. On Kieran's second trip, we went to Nepal and took the backpack rather than the stroller. He was eight months by this time and we did much more walking. For this trip the backpack was more useful with the drawback that he couldn't sleep quite so comfortably in the carrier and it couldn't be used as a chair/restrainer in the restaurant. There are makes of backpacks that can sit up by themselves.

Backpacks may be less useful if you are alone. If your child starts screaming while in the backpack, and you are on your own, it is less easy to pacify. If there are two of you, one can drop back and talk, give a drink or distract them; if you are on your own you have to stop and get them out, which may be difficult. It is always more awkward if you try to use public transport. Getting on and off buses or trains and getting seated is usually easier if you carry the baby in your arms and the backpack separately.

There is now a backpack/stroller on the market which may make life easier. It folds down into a backpack with retractable wheels, and, with a bit of fiddling, springs into action as a stroller – quite ingenious.

Walking & Trekking

Trekking has increased dramatically in popularity, particularly in Nepal where many trekking companies offer family treks. These are generally very well organised and able to deal with quite small children, though they usually have an age limit. Trekking on your own in Nepal with your children is also very easy, if you take into consideration your children's and your own needs when planning the trip. With small children don't plan to go too high or too far. No matter how experienced a walker you are, very young children do not acclimatise to high altitudes as easily as adults and serious problems can result. Altitude sickness can be fatal, even a minor case should be taken seriously.

There are many other walks in Nepal which will be suited to children of all ages. You can hire porters who will carry your packs and your children, and there are many books and agencies available that can give you good advice. In Kathmandu trekking shops and agencies abound, and they can put you on the right track for hiring porters. With small children who are not yet walking, you have to carry the usual equipment. In many areas of Nepal it is not necessary to carry a tent and camping gear as there are hotels, resthouses and restaurants where you can stay and eat all along the route, but it is a good idea to carry your own sleeping bags and a container for water.

Older children, from crawlers to toddlers, may be carried most of the way, but do give them time to do whatever it is they are doing, whether it be crawling in the grass for a while beside the track or toddling along by themselves – it is a trip for them too, and they need to get their turn.

Children who are walking may get bored and want to be carried a lot. Children always enjoy it more when there are others their own age around so it may be a good idea to try to organise a trek with other families.

You need to protect against the elements – sun, cold, etc – and to carry lots of snacks and drinks with you. In cooler weather blanket sleepers make good walking clothes for small children. Add a hood, mittens and a sleeveless jacket and the child is cosy from head to food, and comfortable. If you are planning a cold-weather trek make sure the child's shoes will fit over the plastic 'feet' in the blanket sleeper. Shoes should be comfortable over warm socks. Many experienced walkers recommend tennis shoes or slip-on rubber boots with felt insoles.

Most children like to carry their own packs. These don't have to be expensive, but do have to be light and easy to carry. Children from three years of age can carry their own but there will certainly be some passing it on to Mum or Dad. Check that there are no uncomfortable lumps, let them carry their own snacks and drinks, a flashlight and one or two favourite toys.

The half-length sleeping bags used by climbers are ideal for children and much better quality than the average child size sleeping bag, although these are probably fine for warm weather trekking. If you haven't hired a porter to carry your child, be prepared to do the carrying for a fair proportion of the trip; children tire easily. Obviously for babies and young children a carrier will be essential, while older but still portable children may ride comfortably on their parent's shoulders, or a back carrier could be improvised by organising a 'seat' on your regular backpack.

Don't try to cover as much ground as you would without children. This sounds obvious, but you would be surprised how often parents overlook the obvious. Lots of rest stops are necessary, and bear in mind too that during the rest stops you will have to keep working – entertaining, feeding, washing, whatever. Children are a never-ending source of things to do! Always carry an extra set of clothes in an easily accessible spot. Even amongst the mountains children will be able to find the one puddle of water or mud hole for miles around.

Dress your children in brightly coloured clothes so they are always easy to spot, and it is a good idea to pin a whistle to their jacket, so they can signal you if necessary.

Travellers' Tales

SOUTHERN ASIA

BALI

Of all the places we've taken our kids I think one of the best has been Bali. It's simply a wonderful place to go with kids; not only do they enjoy it but it also opens their eyes to another way of life. Most of our travel in Bali with our children has been staying at quite ordinary cold water *losmen* (small Balinese hotels).

We first took our two to Bali in '83 when Tashi was two and Kieran was only four months old. It was hard work, as travel with very small children always is, but still highly enjoyable. We started off with a few days in Kuta Beach, rented a small Suzuki jeep and went up to Ubud where we became friendly with a Balinese family running a small losmen. Their youngest daughter Ketut has become a real friend to our children and

they have looked forward to seeing her again on every subsequent trip. We continued to the north coast where we stayed in a place called *Nirwana*, a losmen with an absolutely perfect set up for a family – a two-storey room where Maureen and I slept upstairs while the kids were down below, heard but not seen.

In '85 we went to Bali again. Tashi was now four and Kieran was two. Again we started and finished the trip at Kuta Beach, staying in the positively delightful *Poppies Cottages*. The children were now old enough to leave with babysitters – one of Bali's delights. They have a great time with your children, your children have a great time with them. Any losmen can organise one for you and they don't cost a lot. Those romantic candle-lit Balinese dinners, impossible on our first with-the-kids trip to Bali, started to happen again.

In Ubud this time we stayed at the *Ubud Inn*, another beautifully designed upstairs-downstairs place, ideal for families with children. Again we spent a lot of time with our Balinese friends and Tashi was off with Ketut at every opportunity. From there we travelled to Candidasa, the newer Balinese beach resort, and again we found a losmen with a mezzanine sleeping arrangement.

In '88 we were back in Bali again, our children now seven and four-almost-five. We had a spell at *Poppies* where a wonderful swimming pool had been added since our previous visit, much to our aquatic children's delight. In Ubud we stayed with our friends but at their home. From there we rented a small minibus and went to Candidasa and up to the north coast. We stayed at the delightful *Tandjung Sari* hotel at Sanur Beach, one of the few times we've stayed in a place with hot water in Bali, and once again we closed the trip at *Poppies*. Our love affair with Bali continued.[3]

It's the fact that there's so much for children to participate in which makes Bali so much fun. On the first visit we used to have breakfast in the same little *warung* (a sort of Indonesian snack bar) in Ubud every morning. We'd sit there, right by the roadside, eating fruit salad or black rice pudding, with the children calling out *selamat pagi* (good morning) to whoever came by.

Every visit we've managed to go to some Balinese dances. The stories are eternal ones; good versus bad, bad looks like it's going to win, but good turns the tables and eventually emerges triumphant. The baddies really look like baddies – the evil witch Rangda with her bulging eyes and long fingernails is a good example – and the goodies look like goodies. Kids love it and soon learn the stories; they've learnt to like something very real about another culture painlessly.

Even everyday life is fun. Bali is full of spirits – good ones and bad ones – and each morning you have to make offerings to keep the good ones happy and the bad ones in their place. Everywhere you go in Bali you see tiny woven palm trays with a couple of flower petals and a few grains of rice. They're placed on shrines for good spirits or thrown derisively in the road for the bad ones. An offering like this placed by the front door is to persuade bad spirits to take the bribe and not come in. Every morning in Ubud Tashi would go down to the market with Ketut to buy the little offering trays and then put them out around the house. We noticed, however, that Ketut usually took care of the good spirits while Tashi was left to handle the baddies!

At Candidasa last trip I got a fisherman to take us out to the reef, about half a km offshore, in his outrigger. Kieran's swimming (he was only four) was still a bit shaky but with the outrigger to hang on to he had no trouble getting a good look at the fish even though his diving mask was a pretty sloppy fit.

Of course travelling with children in Bali also has its problems. Some good friends of ours, also regular visitors with their kids, made their first visit just as their son, William, was cutting his first teeth. Everybody they met would point at him and comment on his *gigi* (teeth). By the time they left they'd actually started to call him Gigi and now, three years and another trip to Bali later, he's known as Gigi to everybody! I doubt he'll ever become Bill.

Tony Wheeler

INDONESIA

In early '88 we made our third trip with the children to Bali but also fitted in a couple of weeks travelling around Java. Our travels started in Yogyakarta, the cultural centre of Indonesia, where our small hotel had a small swimming pool – a luxury that with children sometimes approaches being a necessity. When it's hot and dusty and there's simply been too much sightseeing there is nothing like a pool for instant mood changing.

Yogya, as it's known, offers plenty of child-size treats, including the complicated maze-like ruins of the old water palace and most definitely bicycle-rickshaws. It's one of those Asian towns where the cycle-rickshaw is absolutely the number one form of transport and the cycle-rickshaw drivers are often cheerful characters. One night we had gone to a restaurant that put on a traditional puppet show during the meal and afterwards emerged to find a rickshaw to get home with. You often see whole families and baggage too piled high on one overloaded rickshaw but we and our kids are probably somewhat heavier than the average Indonesian equivalents so we decided to take two rickshaws; one for Maureen and Kieran, one for Tashi and me. Our rickshaw jockeys decided this was a great opportunity for a cycle-rickshaw grand prix and for the next 20 minutes we scorched through the quiet streets of late night Yogya, our kids enthusiastically cheering them on.

From Yogya we took a minibus to Cirebon from where we made the interesting 'backwater' boat trip to Pangandaran. It's one of those trips you're glad you've made because now you won't have to do it again! Cooped up on a tightly packed boat we'd probably seen all we wanted to see of Indonesian river-boats by the time we arrived. Pangandaran with its beaches, jungle clad headland and interesting fish market was a good break from the cities before we finished off our Java visit with Bandung, Bogor and Jakarta.

Bandung's highlight was a visit to the simmering volcano of Tangkuban Prahu but Dunia Fantasi in Jakarta was undoubtedly the highlight of the whole trip for the kids. The name means Fantasy World and it's nothing less than a pretty good miniature Disneyland – all those popular rides at a fraction of the western price. Well there were a few power cuts and the mystery ice cream flavour did turn out to be durian, but otherwise there were no complaints!

Tony Wheeler

NEPAL, INDIA & SRI LANKA

In late '83, when Tashi was about to turn three and Kieran was still less than a year we set off on a trip to the sub-continent. I was already in Bangkok so I met Maureen and the children there and Tashi, who hadn't seen me for a couple of weeks, spotted me from the customs hall and shot straight past the inspection counter and out the door; she definitely had nothing to declare!

Maureen and I had visited Kathmandu on a number of occasions in the past and it remains one of our favourite cities, so we felt at home straight away. To the children it was definitely a little unusual at first and it's a good illustration of how travel with children opens, or re-opens, your eyes to unusual things that have become commonplace. After numerous visits to India seeing cows wander city streets is not at all unusual to us, but we had hardly been in Kathmandu an hour on this visit before this utterly amazing sight, cows wandering between the cars and buses, was pointed out to us by a fresh pair of eyes!

And there were plenty of other equally amazing sights. On our way to breakfast in the morning we might see a potter turning out instantly disposable little clay drinking cups. Monkeys performed gymnastics, sliding down the bannisters on the steps up the Swayambhunath pagoda. When a monkey urinated on the head of a Nepalese passing under an archway near the Pashupatinath temple he ruefully admitted that he had been 'blessed by Hanuman' (Hanuman is the monkey god).

Bicycling is a favourite way of exploring the Kathmandu Valley and we had basketware bicycle seats made up and did some riding with the kids on the back. Tashi and Kieran were too young for trekking at this stage, of course, but with Kieran in a carrypack and Tashi often riding on my shoulders we did some short walks in the valley and spent a few days in Dhulikhel from where we did a pleasant day walk to the village of Panauti. We took the bus to Pokhara and did some more short day walks there and boated around the lake. And right at the end of our stay Tashi celebrated her third birthday with a little party in our hotel garden and a cake from *KC's Restaurant* with Tashi written in English, Sanskrit and Tibetan – Tashi is a Tibetan name of course.

From Kathmandu we made the short flight down to Calcutta and spent a few days staying with a good Indian friend before heading south again to Sri Lanka. In Sri Lanka we rented a small car and visited the highlands, the ancient cities and the wonderful beaches around the coast. A highlight of this part of the trip was the elephant orphanage just outside Kandy. When an elephant is only shoulder height to a three year old it's a quite delightful creature, you don't even complain too much if it inadvertently steps on your foot.

Tony Wheeler

On the Road

WHAT TO TAKE

I won't attempt to make a comprehensive list of everything you should bring, since everyone has different needs. I will try to catalogue all the things that I have found made life a bit easier either for me or the kids.

The first rule of thumb is to take as little as possible. Keep paring it down to where you think it isn't nearly enough – it almost always is. Remember, in general babies' needs are pretty simple and wherever you go people have babies, so you can usually improvise.

Clothes

Cotton is really the only material that can be worn comfortably in the tropics. Children really don't need too many clothes, nor clothes that are too fancy – shorts and T-shirts are ideal. For babies just a T-shirt and nappy are enough. A warm sweater and a waterproof jacket or suit should cover most contingencies. These are the tropical basics; what you feel you must have is up to you. Underwear should also be cotton and make sure pants don't rub around the top of the legs; they should be a little loose there because when the child gets sweaty tight leg bands can cause a rash or fungal infection. A medicated powder or baby powder is also useful on areas that get sweaty.

Although your children will probably want to run around bare-foot this is not a good idea in many Third World countries. Light sandals, thongs, or some such protection should be worn at all times. There are various worm infections which enter through the skin of the feet, and as the beaches, paths, pavements, tracks, in fact almost the entire surface of some Third World countries, will be dotted with animal and human faeces and other undesirable elements, it is a good idea to insist that your children wear some-thing on their feet at all times.

In many countries it is advisable to wear some sort of footwear when paddling in the sea, or wading through rock pools, to protect from sharp coral or shells and any creatures that may be lurking. There are many suitable shoes, plastic, open sandals, thongs or light canvas shoes.

Nappies Let me now break the bad news. Nappies, diapers, call them what you will, are non-existent in many parts of the Third World. So is nappy rash. In general when Third World babies are very small they have old cloths underneath them when they are lying down, and these are changed when necessary. When they are carried cloths are sort of packed under them, not really fastened, just placed strategically. Once on a long bus trip in India a woman beside me had a very tiny, new baby on her knee; she had the cloth arrangement and also managed to cup her hands under the child at appropriate moments and scoop the collected liquid out the window!

At a few months they often wear cotton pants, and when damp-ness or anything else seeps through, the person carrying the baby holds them out over a gutter or field or wherever and then changes the pants. When they are old enough to toddle they very sensibly go bare-arsed until they are to be trusted. When they get the urge they just go wherever they may be. None of which is very helpful to us travelling westerners.

Your child can probably do without nappies quite a lot of the time. If you spend a while on the beaches, or stay at any one place for a while, no one will mind if they do like the locals. However at night, when travelling, or when shopping, some protection will be necessary. And I'm afraid there is no really easy way.

You could try and carry cloth nappies – these are easy to pack – but unless you plan to stay in one place for quite some time, not really practical. For a start they have to be soaked and sterilised, for which you need a bucket. You can get collapsible buckets for camping, but then you have to carry the sterilising solution, and you will not find any gracing the shelves of the stores in most Asian towns and villages. You have to be in a place long enough to soak, wash and dry. You may find that the climate will not be conducive to the wearing of plastic pants. Also you will have to carry quite a few nappies, and when they get dirty you have to stow them some place until you can soak them. Despite all that, I have met people travelling with babies and cloth nappies and they seemed to manage.

I carried masses of disposable nappies. I calculated how many nappies I use at home per day, multiplied by the number of days I'll be away, added an extra two a day for emergencies and also brought a few cloth nappies with separate waterproof pants as an extra precaution. We would leave home with one large bag full of nappies. As they were used up, the bag became free to carry purchases. Disposable nappies are light and pack down easily, so they don't really affect your luggage allowance, they're just bulky. Where possible I let the children disport themselves as nature intended, which conserved the nappies somewhat. It's vital to carry a roll of tape for when the tabs fail as you can't afford to waste them.

Since most disposable nappies my children have ever used are not really adequate for night use, I place a 'diaper doubler' (US name), which is just a soft disposable pad, inside the nappy. This helps keep the child dry at night. In Britain you can buy rolls of disposable nappies which you cut to fit. In Australia I used the type of disposable nappy which has to be fitted into plastic pants, the new-born size is about right for fitting into most disposable nappies.

Disposing of the nappies is something that bothers me somewhat. There is no garbage collection in much of Third World Asia and very often garbage finds its way into the streets or alleyways. I carry plastic bin bags and leave a full, sealed one behind for the hotel to dispose of. I never leave them anywhere else and I just hope the hotel disposes of them properly. Getting to the toilet trained stage is the single biggest step towards easier travelling with children and we were very pleased when Kieran made that important step soon after we arrived in Bali on his second visit there.

Disposable nappies are very much a First World creation but these days you can find them in many Third World or developing nations although, of course, they're principally there for visitors rather than local consumption.

Asia In Asia the advanced nations like Japan, Singapore and Hong Kong will have nappies readily available. They can be found in major towns or tourist centres in Malaysia, the Philippines, Thailand and Indonesia, with difficulty in large cities in India (try the Childcare Chain stores), and in Colombo in Sri Lanka. In Kathmandu, Nepal, there is a supermarket called the Bluebird Stores by the Bagmati Bridge on the Kathmandu side which sells various baby products (including disposable nappies) but they are very expensive. Outside Kathmandu you will not find much. In Burma, forget it. China may begin to produce such luxuries but for now bring your own.

South America Generally available in big cities in most countries in Central and South America, more widely available in countries like Brazil.

Africa Widely available in South Africa and Zimbabwe and in main centres in touristed countries like Kenya. Very difficult in the less developed countries.

You can try asking the airline of the country you are visiting or the national tourist office but be fairly sceptical of their information. If you need disposable nappies you are much better bringing them with you. Apart from the certainty of actually having them they will also be much cheaper back home in the west.

HOTELS & SLEEPING
Some children will sleep anywhere with a minimum of fuss. At one stage my children certainly did not fit into that category although they are much better now they are a bit older. If your children are members of the great non-sleepers conspiracy there are a number of possible solutions.

Your children may not take to too much moving around. You may find that they find it hard to settle in a new room. It may be worthwhile to make sure you are always settled into the hotel early in the afternoon to give your children time to get used to it. Even very young babies can be extremely sensitive to their surroundings. Try to give them time to explore the room, play in it, learn where the bathroom is, etc. It is also an idea to carry something which will make the room familiar. With older children set out their toys and books. Let them choose a drawer or space to put their clothes in. Let them play house. Little boys and girls love to bustle around 'tidying up' and each new room can provide an excellent opportunity. If they want to move things, let them (within reason). Try to have something that a baby can always have within view; a small hanging object, a fluffy toy that sits on the bed, a familiar rug or cuddly will help children settle.

The fact that you are all sleeping in the same room may also be unsettling for your children. I find that the younger they are, the more difficult it is. Tashi will now sleep through anything, yet as a baby the slightest noise would have her awake and noisy. Babies tend to sleep lightly and are easily disturbed. When there are four of you you may find it easier, and if you're budget travelling not very expensive, to take two rooms side by side, rather than all pile into one. In some places, like Bali, you can often get two rooms sharing a verandah, and this can quickly assume a very homelike atmosphere, with the verandah becoming your private 'sitting room'. You also have the benefit of two bathrooms. It's surprising how often even pretty basic hotels have some sort of family room or 'suite'. Getting a place where you have your space and the children have theirs can make a real difference to everybody's comfort.

Daytime naps can be a problem. Small children need them and may quite happily sleep on your shoulder wherever you may be. Others may require to be laid down on a bed, given a drink and a cuddle before they can drift off. When Tashi was two we spent an hour or so every afternoon lying beside her telling her stories and singing songs before she would go to sleep. You can sometimes make a choice; keep your children awake all afternoon, and put them to bed early (which means your day ends early too) or insist that they have an afternoon nap and then hopefully they will be fresh for longer at night and you can take them with you when you go out to eat, without exhaustion making the experience a misery for all of you.

When I say you have a choice, I am assuming your children will comply – they don't always. It was always a battle to get Tashi to sleep and from the day she was born sleep was something she tried to do without. When she was 18 months she gave up all daytime naps but got into the habit of going to bed at 6 to 6.30 pm and sleeping a straight 12 hours. We found that when she was little we stuck to that routine when travelling and it worked quite well. From age two, however, we found that the travelling and the heat tired her out, so that we could get her to go to sleep in the afternoon (with songs, etc!) and she would stay up quite late, quite happily.

Kieran however, was quite a different kettle of fish. He would sleep until midnight after which he would wake for a chat at least once before dawn. He liked to have a good morning sleep, in a bed, and then until he was 13 months, again in the afternoon. Which meant that our days had to be structured around his naps. This was sometimes awkward, and at times he just had to accept that bed was not available, but on the whole we tried to keep to the routine he liked. On his first trip, when he was just four months and he was more able to sleep anywhere, we took a reclining stroller and he would sleep in that. However, where possible, we did try to do it his way.

As he got older it was more difficult; no matter how tired he got, if he couldn't lie down and have a sleep, he was miserable and quite able to keep himself awake way beyond the point where he could cope. It is not worth trying to force your children to 'get used to it' in this sort of situation; you will simply have to organise your travelling to suit them. This is where the compromise comes in – you have to, your children won't.

Older children are much easier; they usually like new hotel rooms, and will run around sussing out what they offer. Usually they have a preferred bed to sleep on within minutes of entering the room, and they also like to set out their toys and books and make a space for themselves. Going to bed at night is the usual matter of getting them to settle down, but they usually present few problems as the days' events will have worn them out. Tony and I like to have a room with a verandah or some separate space where we can sit and read or talk while the children eventually go to sleep. This isn't always possible, so you are stuck with trying to dim the room sufficiently to encourage the children to sleep but not so much that you are forced to go to bed too. As the children get older you may find that they can stay awake until reasonably late, and then you can all go to bed at the same time.

Cribs/Cots

Expensive 'international standard' hotels can almost always supply them and in many places even more reasonably priced places will have something for a baby or small child to sleep in. Some places will charge more for a cot but many cheap places will not have heard of them; in the Third World even many medium priced hotels will look at you with incomprehension.

For very small babies you can get portable carry-cots which airlines will carry free. Some quite sophisticated baby sleeping paraphernalia is available but travelling with a baby you have to carry so much extra luggage already that you may prefer to simply cope as you go along. In many places in the world you could always get something made if you're going to be staying around long enough or find that life without a carry-cot is impossible. We met a family in Bali once who had a beautiful cane one made up.

I didn't carry a bed with me for either of the children, and although it would have been useful at times we managed without one. There are all sorts of alternatives including the children simply sleeping with you although if your children are restless sleepers, like Tashi was, that can be no fun at all.

Two arm chairs placed facing each other can make a fine, safe sleeping cot for a small child. Even if you don't leave him there all night it can be useful for putting him to sleep during the day, when

you don't want to go to bed with him, and also for the first part of
the evening when he is asleep, but the rest of you are sitting up
reading or whatever. A large drawer might also prove serviceable
as an improvised cot.

Children from 18 months onwards (depending on how big they
are and how confident) can really go into a bed. You can always
make sure they get the one against the wall and put a pillow beside
them if you worry about them falling out.

What to Carry for Sleeping

For bedding you need two cotton sheets, one warm blanket, a
mosquito net (in the tropics), a lambskin or similar 'cuddly'. Of
course you don't need to provide all your own bedding but lambskins are a very good idea in that even if the baby sweats a lot, they
never feel really damp. They are always soft and cuddly and keep
a child warm when they are cold and cool when they are hot. You
can use lambskins under the sheet as well as on top of it. They are
washable but you need a full, hot day to dry them.

For small babies cotton sleeping bags (the type that go on like a
nightgown over the head and arms, but fasten down the middle and
are sewn along the bottom like a bag) are cooler than sleepsuits,
but protect the child from draughts and mosquitoes. Only a soft,
light cotton material is necessary. Perhaps (again for small babies)

a knitted, woollen bag, or one of the quilted 'pouches' would be a good idea if you plan to go to cooler climates.

Waterproof sheeting is a very good idea for all small children. Even reliably toilet trained little ones can have an occasional failure when they're very tired or in strange surroundings. Hotels, even cheap ones, generally take this in their stride but you will probably feel better if you carry your own protection. I usually took the terry/rubber backed type of cot sheet and put it under the sheet. I found it tended to get less hot and sticky than having straight plastic under the sheet. The only problem is remembering to take it with you when you leave the hotel, we 'almost' left ours behind on many occasions. It's worth having a check list of important things and ticking it off before you lock the bags.

I did hear of one family who carried an inflatable mattress for their child to sleep on in order to protect the beds, but I think that may not be too comfortable if you have a child who likes to travel around the bed while asleep. Tashi would have spent most of the night on the floor.

Bathing

This may sound very simple but, depending on the age of your child, it may require some organisation, particularly if you are travelling on a budget or off the beaten track and your room does not have an attached bathroom, or there is no bath in the bathroom. Sometimes, as in Indonesia, even a western-type shower may not be available. Most children under 12 months are not quite ready for an Indonesian *mandi* – standing in the bathroom sloshing buckets of cold water over their heads – come to that, a great many adults aren't either! You can often ask for hot water to bathe a small child in but it can take some time to produce and in tropical areas where nobody washes in hot water you will be looked at somewhat askance! The hotel may also have a tin bath, or a plastic basin you can borrow.

One place we stayed at in Pokhara, Nepal had two plastic basins for washing clothes. I bathed Tashi and Kieran on the grass outside, in the hottest part of the day because the water was cold, by sitting them in one each and scrubbing them down. They thought it was great fun. Tashi at two thought Indonesian mandis were great, but her feet were the only part of her that really got washed. Now both children love them and have great fun hurling water around and shrieking with pleasure. Staying in *ryokan* (traditional Japanese inns), the Japanese baths where you wash outside the bath, then sit and soak in the hot water, proved an equally big hit.

Some small children will take showers, but most of them do not like the experience of water gushing down on them. When Kieran was really little, I used to just lie him on the plastic change mat I had brought, get a bucket of warmish water and wash him down with a cloth. Even in the tropics it can get very cool when the sun goes down (or at least comparatively cooler) and the children may complain loudly about the cold water, so try and wash them while the day is still pretty warm. Then you can let them splash around as much as they like and hopefully clean them in the process.

For teeth cleaning, keep boiled, purified water in the bathroom and make sure your children know that it must be used when cleaning teeth and for rinsing the toothbrush. Small children often swallow quite a lot of water when cleaning their teeth, so although you may not think it is necessary for yourself, try to make it a rule for the children, and don't let them see you doing otherwise.

Toilets

If your children are past the nappy stage, they may well be at the 'toilet' stage. You know, the one where they can't pass up the opportunity to use a different toilet no matter where she might be? I remember having to swiftly curtail Tashi's delight at being let loose in a showroom full of new bathroom fittings. With both our children there was a phase where no restaurant visit (or flight for that matter) was complete without a thorough inspection of the sanitary facilities.

If, however, toilet facilities are not conveniently to hand and your child gets caught short, any restaurant, coffee shop or hotel will let you use their bathrooms in an emergency, whether you are a patron or not. In small towns or villages, if there is an absence of public places, you can always explain the situation to a pleasant looking bystander (you will almost always have an entourage around you). Whether or not you will always want to use the facilities offered, is another question. If you are absolutely stuck, do what the locals do, hold your child out over a drain, or any other likely place.

In parts of Asia where toilets are usually of the squat down rather than familiar, western sit-up variety your children may baulk at these 'hole in the ground' affairs. Try to be patient, I'll bet you did too when you first saw them. If you show them how it's done, they'll probably come to regard it at least as an interesting novelty. Always go with them and help them to get organised – they will probably want to be held while they are squatting, many children are afraid they are about to disappear down the hole.

FOOD
Breast Feeding

Babies are easy. There is only one way to feed a travelling baby and that is with the breast. I have read in some book on travelling with children that nursing mothers may lose or deplete their milk supply while travelling. I suppose the idea is that it is tiring and anxiety provoking. Well it may be but I don't know of any mother yet who has had this happen to her, and I can't think of anything more tiring or anxiety-causing than trying to feed a child with a bottle and formula while travelling. How would you keep the bottle sterile? How would you get it to the right temperature while travelling on a bus in Java? How do you make up the formula with the necessary clean water? What happens when your baby wants a drink on the road, or in a hotel bedroom at 3 am? How do you keep the formula good in a humid climate without a fridge? The mind boggles.

If you are travelling with a baby under 12 months old – you have got to breast feed. One way you can ensure your milk supply does not diminish is to feed whenever the baby seems to want to drink. This will probably be very frequently. I found that the best way of dealing with night feeds was to take the baby into bed with me and just let them get on with it, I was vaguely aware during the night when they fed, but I didn't need to become totally conscious and it wasn't nearly so tiring.

Don't try to race around and see everything in a hurry. Go easy on yourself, slow down, then you will be less tired and more relaxed. Drink lots of fluid and make sure you eat properly. All the usual advice to nursing mothers applies when you are travelling. Since most mothers are not likely to be taking brand new babies travelling (I think three months is probably early enough), you shouldn't have to worry about what you eat. I love curries and ate what I felt like, and it didn't seem to bother either Tashi or Kieran, although they may have become acclimatised in the womb! Nor will it affect the child if you have a stomach upset, although you must be extremely careful not to pass it on due to lack of hygiene. Make sure you wash your hands thoroughly, and frequently.

Solid Food

When your baby requires a few extras in the food line you can generally find plenty to suit. Mashed bananas can be prepared almost anywhere and scrambled eggs are just about always available. A lot of Chinese food is suitable for children; steamed chicken, sweet corn and chicken soup – for very young babies watch the corn. I found that Tashi at six months just loved Chinese food and managed to find out for herself what she liked. She used to just help herself from my plate, but became a little more cautious after trying a mouthful of curry.

Obviously you have to be careful about bones, but apart from avoiding choking your child don't be too dogmatic about what they can and can't eat. Indian children are introduced to spices from an early age, which doesn't mean that you can start sprinkling chilli on your baby's scrambled egg. If you let them help themselves whenever they show interest you will soon find what they will and won't eat.

I have never used the commercially-prepared baby foods at home, but I did carry a few jars as a back-up when we travelled and once or twice they were useful. There are also dried food preparations which have to be mixed with hot water or milk.

Cereals are often a very useful stand-by to have with you. These are easy to pack and keep, but you will have to be careful to use properly boiled/sterilised water or milk when making them up too. You can often buy these in the kind of stores that will have disposable nappies.

Drinking

In parts of the world where the water is not safe to drink unless it has been boiled or properly purified, the usual advice to adults is to drink tea or coffee or commercial brands of bottled drinks. None of this advice is much use to small children. Babies are not very enthusiastic about tea or coffee and you have long years ahead trying to persuade them not to drink too many Cokes; you don't want to start them on that habit at six months of age.

Fortunately in recent years those small individual cartons of fruit drinks, complete with sealed straw, have become familiar almost throughout the world. They make a great safe alternative to soft drinks and are easily transportable so if you're travelling in a remote region it's a good idea to stock up on them when you find them.

You can also make fruit juice yourself by squeezing oranges, either by hand or with a plastic squeezer/juicer and you should always have a water bottle with boiled, purified water with you. In many places fresh fruit juices that you can see being made are available, just make sure they don't add ice or water unless you know it's OK.

If your child drinks from a bottle carry two small plastic bottles and nipples and some sterilizing tablets. Each night you can ask your hotel or restaurant for some boiled water. I found that an empty, cylindrical Johnson's Baby Wipe container, thoroughly cleaned, was just big enough to make an ideal sterilizing unit – fill with water, add the tab and bottle and nipple, put the lid on and leave overnight.

When they're a bit older the soft drinks alternative does come in. You may not be happy having your children drink too many of them but reputable major brands of soft drinks are produced under hygienic conditions and are quite safe. It is, however, easy to fall into the soft drinks trap, where you end up buying soft drinks several times a day because it is hot and at least the drinks are safe. We try to stick to a one-soft-drink-a-day rule; the rest of the time it is juice or our own treated water, possibly flavoured with powder. The children accept this and look forward to their 'treat' and we find that they will often decide for themselves they don't really want a soft drink, especially where there are good fresh juices. Forbidding soft drinks completely is difficult when you are exposed to them so often (eating in restaurants, etc) and gives the children something else to complain about when they feel grumpy.

Milk is not as widely available or drunk as much in the Third World as it is in the West, although even in India it is often possible to find. Where it is not pre-packaged it is usually just boiled and served hot, or with a chunk of ice to cool it down. I have drunk it often, especially when I was pregnant, but only freshly boiled milk is safe and avoid the ice. Third World cows are not always well cared for and the person milking the animal may not observe strict hygienic habits, or may not be very healthy. The storage and transportation of the milk may also be suspect.

These days in South-East Asia in particular and increasingly in other parts of the world you will find cartons of long-life milk, plain or flavoured. This is fine and can be a real life saver with young children. Soy bean milk is also available in cartons in South-East Asia.

Where You Eat

Even in the most remote places small local restaurants will be quite happy to see children. Even the open-air stall in a small town in Malaysia will have a high chair which proprietors will produce with a flourish when they see you coming. In fact in some Third World or developing countries they will do everything other than actually feed your child. I don't know how many times Tashi or Kieran were taken away for a walk to see the relatives while I ate my meal in peace. Nor do most small places mind the mess; lots of little street front restaurants in Asia just have concrete floors

which they can brush straight on to the street. Besides, what self-respecting Chinese would expect anyone to eat without making a mess?

Nevertheless, you may find that you have to eat at more expensive restaurants or in the more expensive hotels more often than you might wish. Small children are notoriously unadventurous in their eating habits and you may have to pass up some wonderful local eating opportunities while you search for some place that can produce an imitation of a mundane cheese and tomato sandwich or a hot dog. Having said that, beware of the hot dogs that look wonderful but with the first bite bring a howl of pained disbelief because the 'tomato sauce' is really chilli, and the 'spaghetti bolognese' that bears no earthly resemblance in taste to what your children (and you) are used to. No matter how they are described on the menu you will to some extent just have to cross your fingers and hope. A quick rule of thumb is the bigger and flashier the hotel, the more 'authentic' the western food will be.

It is a good idea to give in to these demands for familiar food from time to time. If you try too rigidly to stick to an eating budget, or insist that you eat local food 'because you can always get a sandwich at home, and when in Thailand eat what the Thais eat' you will find yourself with a rebellious child whose determination is usually greater than yours.

There have been occasions when the children have noticed the local equivalent of 'Burger King' or 'Kentucky Fried Chicken' and despite the different language have recognised them instantly. Tony and I retain our ideological purity by letting the children eat there, then they have to come and watch us eat at a place of our choice, and afterwards we find common ground on dessert!

Unfamiliar food or not, there are some great dining possibilities which children will love. In Japan eating out is made much easier by the plastic versions of what you can expect to eat inside, displayed in the window of the restaurant. While it certainly makes ordering easy you may have to dissuade your child from ordering the most luridly coloured dishes. Remind them they have to eat them as well as look at them!

One seafood restaurant we visited several times in Sri Lanka provided endless interest with its corral of crabs, awaiting their fate. In Singapore and in other parts of Asia many Chinese restaurants have virtual aquariums of fish, prawns and other extremely fresh dining possibilities. The chef spinning out noodles on the spot had our kids enthralled at a restaurant in Hong Kong and what child could resist a Mongolian hot pot or Korean barbecue where you cook the food yourself, Swiss fondue style, right on the table. While all this may be fun, the children may still not eat.

We've had some wonderful children's food surprises over the years. All over the sub-continent producing amazing cakes is a real art. Tashi had a marvellous third birthday cake baked in Kathmandu; it was a vision in mustard yellow, candy pink and lime green with icing flowers, three candles and 'Happy Birthday' in English and Nepali.

Eating in restaurants is a mixed pleasure with children. Usually children enjoy eating out, but it does require a fairly sensible attitude. Choose restaurants that are not too crowded, possibly by eating earlier you can miss the crowds. Check the menu to make sure there is something your children can eat. If there isn't a high chair and you have to have a child on your knee, don't order soup.

Carry spout cups for small children to have their drinks from, this can save a lot of spills. If they refuse to be seen drinking from spout cups, teach them to drink through straws which they can usually manage from an early age. Always carry a mop-up cloth, bibs, wet wipes and other cleaning apparatus. It helps to have your own plate and spoon, so that you can organise a small portion for your child without having to wait for the waiter to bring you what you need, or go through the sometimes frustrating task of trying to get him to understand that you really want an extra empty plate.

Older children make for easier dining companions, but in general the amount of food served in restaurants is too much for a small child, a sandwich may sound fine but it can come with chips (French fries) and salad which remain untouched. Entrees (appetisers) are often the right amount of food for children, or sharing a meal between two can work out if both people can agree on what to share! Tony and I often order three dishes for four of us and then everyone takes what they want (in some restaurants two meals are adequate).

Compromise is a necessary attribute for travelling families, but really it is the parents who have to compromise. Your children would be perfectly happy to stay home; this trip is your idea. If you want them to have a positive attitude towards travel you must meet them halfway. You can always go without a meal but your children can't. If your children are feeling a little bit homesick, familiar food can help to allay the feeling that home has disappeared. A splurge on a milk shake or ice cream can often work wonders and is well worth the money spent.

I remember one particularly miserable trip in Java, Indonesia. There were endless hours in a crowded, slow and very uncomfortable bemo. We finally arrived at a rather gloomy hotel in Bandung just as it began to pour with rain. We were all tired, fed up and rather cranky. Tony went out and scouted around while I tried to cheer up the children; after a little while he was back with the news that we were close to a great place to eat and several cake shops. Off we went: a good spaghetti bolognese, pizza, soft drink, followed by a visit to the cake shops, then back to the hotel carrying three little boxes of disgusting looking cakes, to find that there was a video showing *Teenwolf* with Michael J Fox. It all had absolutely nothing to do with why you go to Java but the day had been completely turned around and the kids thought Bandung was terrific!

Try not to worry if you think your children are just not eating enough. There may be days when you think they are living on air but they probably do that at home as well, so don't start worrying that this trip will end with starved, malnourished children. Children eat when they are hungry. As long as you make an effort to find things that they can eat, and should like, given their own taste, you can't do any more. Carry some children's multi-vitamin drops or tablets, make sure they drink a lot, offer them fruit and after that relax.

Alternatives

There are occasions when a restaurant is not a good idea: when you have been out all afternoon, and now it's dinner time and the baby is tired, and you all feel a bit strained and hungry. An older child may express their misery with a continuous aggravating whine. This is not the time to be shushing them and pointing out that the whole restaurant is watching, that will only raise the decibel level. At times like this a quiet meal in your room can be a terrific alternative.

Room service is one way of doing it. The inflated prices and sometimes mediocre food which seem to come with room service are nothing compared to the joy of not having to set out to find a restaurant, find something everyone can eat, keep the children awake and happy through the process of ordering and waiting for food to arrive and then persuade them to eat something. Children usually really enjoy room service (little hedonists) and if it is kept for those special occasions, the idea of a 'treat' may cheer them up completely. In the privacy of your room they can eat how they like, in their pyjamas perhaps, ready to go to bed right after. There will be a mess of course, so try to avoid eating on the beds.

Even cheap hotels can usually send someone out for you. In Asia there always seems to be a local restaurant or cafe just around the corner where the hotel staff send out for noodles or tea, eating out is quite a corner-stone of Asian life and take-aways probably were invented here!

Alternatively one of the parents can go on a food-gathering mission to a local fast food place, a restaurant with take-aways, or even to a night market or food stall. Some places in Asia are quite ingenious at devising take-away packages, as are restaurants and coffee shops. Sometimes you can fix something yourself. Noodles are a great stand-by and most children will eat these. If you have an electric element for boiling water you could always use it to boil some two minute noodles which are available everywhere. Add a few pieces of fruit for dessert and another crisis has been averted!

We have never carried a camping stove but I have had letters from travelling parents who feel that life on the road would have been impossible without one. There are various types on the market, but those that use kerosene or spirit would be more useful than Camping Gaz as you will be able to refill them just about anywhere, and you can empty them out to take on planes, whereas Camping Gaz cylinders may not be widely available and you cannot carry them on planes.

The packets and/or jars of baby food that you have been toting around can prove very useful. Do anything that will fill your child's stomach without subjecting you all to unnecessary stress. It may put paid to your plans for the evening – you may have been dreaming all day of the dinner you would have at a favourite restaurant, you may be very hungry and want a 'real' meal, you may wish you had listened to advice and stayed home – but remember that flexibility is a real attribute for any traveller and an absolute essential for a travelling parent.

Food Rules

The food in the Third World is often basically very good – it certainly won't be shot full of chemicals and preservatives the way so much of ours is. But in many places hygiene leaves a lot to be desired and you do have to be careful, especially with children. What won't affect your stomach may well prove disastrous to your child's less hardened digestive system. The basic rules apply when eating out in the Third World:

Choose only the cleanest-looking restaurants.

Don't feed your child raw salads, or uncooked food. It is best to buy fruit from the market, wash it in purified water and peel it yourself.

Don't use water for adding to juice or washing your babies' utensils unless you know it has been boiled. Always keep a water bottle full of boiled or purified water. For boiled water to be absolutely safe, it has to have been boiled for at least 10 minutes, so if you are in doubt add purifying tabs as an extra precaution.

Wash your own and your child's hands before you eat. Many restaurants will have hand basins with soap and towels and Asians in particular are usually very careful about this aspect of hygiene, although the towels supplied may look rather grotty. If you carry your wet wipes you can clean up whenever necessary.

Milk and other dairy products are not eaten widely in many societies outside the western world. Cheese is available in tins in some countries and you often come across it in places frequented by western travellers. The prepackaged, flavoured yoghurt with which we are familiar is available in many countries and plain yoghurt is a familiar locally made food in places all over the world. All over the sub-continent, where it is known as curd and made from goat's or buffalo's milk, it can be really delicious. In Sri Lanka when you buy curd it comes in an individual pottery container!

Most Asian countries will have tins of baby formula available in familiar western brands. This has been a controversial activity for some years as critics claim that the western companies are pushing their products as a viable alternative to breast feeding, failing to admit that it is never as good as the real thing. In the Third World there is also the very real danger that the formula may be mixed with contaminated water. In less developed countries you should be very careful before using these products as they may not have been stored in ideal conditions. Check the expiry date, ensure it has not been opened, and where it has to be mixed with water be very careful that the water is safe.

While I do think you have to be very careful where your children eat, and endeavour to ensure that everything is hygienically prepared and served, don't become too paranoid. You will soon get a feel for where to eat. Restaurants that are popular and crowded are usually OK, no restaurant lasts for long if it's poisoning its patrons! Restaurants that are crowded with western travellers will also usually be producing food that appeals to western tastes. There seems to be a travellers' menu that has spread throughout the world with familiar features like fruit salad, pancakes, French fries, yoghurt and so on.

Things to Bring for Eating

Babies Bring bottles, teaspoon or baby spoon, plastic dish (wash in boiling water frequently), strainer (tea strainer will do, useful for straining fresh juice), and a plastic juicer. Also, several towelling bibs or a couple of soft plastic ones.

Children Bring a cup with spout, teaspoon (handy when you are only given a large spoon and fork in a restaurant), plastic bowl (for when you put together a meal yourself, or give them a share of yours). Older children don't require any special equipment unless you are in an area where chopsticks only are used.

Despite the availability of high chairs in many restaurants there are many times when they are not available but you would love to have one. For children who can sit up alone, there are fold-up chairs which suspend from the table. The chairs have nylon or plastic seats and are light and reasonably portable. A stroller can also double as a chair in a restaurant.

Miscellaneous Always carry snacks with you, particularly if you are going walking or travelling by bus, train or car. Even if you know there are shops around or the trip is scheduled for just an hour – remember that delays are not unusual and that shops when you arrive may not have anything suitable for your child to eat. So carry sultanas or raisins, nuts, an apple or orange (bananas go mushy very quickly), some water or juice or milk cartons, some bread or biscuits. Carry a knife for peeling and cutting fruit and a few jars of baby food just in case.

Biscuits (cookies) are available just about everywhere and can be a special treat just in case your child is particularly tired and cranky and needs a bit of incentive to go on. Marie biscuits, that venerable English standby, seem to have been left behind in every remote corner of the old British Empire. Children usually like them and you can get them in South-East Asia, on the sub-continent and in Africa. The British Cadbury's brand of chocolates are also found worldwide.

Travellers' Tales

NORTH-EAST ASIA

JAPAN, HONG KONG & MACAU

Coming back from the US to Australia in '85 we spent several weeks in East Asia, starting with Japan. Flying straight from the US west coast to Tokyo is a miserable experience; it's a long, dreary flight virtually directly east-west so the time change is horrific. Tokyo is actually a couple of time zones west of the Australian east coast so it's worse than the longer trans-Pacific flight between the US and Australia.

We arrived in Tokyo early evening, made the long trek into the city from Narita Airport, found our faceless international hotel, had a quick meal and soon couldn't keep our eyes open any longer and fell asleep. Come 1 am, however, Kieran (2½ years old at the time and a long way from being *au fait* with time zones and jet lag) was up and bouncing around. Nobody else was going to sleep with him awake so although I certainly wasn't bouncing anywhere I managed to get dressed and take him to a nearby shopping centre where we window shopped for the next couple of hours and gave Maureen and Tashi a chance to sleep.

We soon left Tokyo and the rest of our visit to Japan was much more traditional. We stayed in *ryokan* rather than in regular hotels and this was one aspect of Japan which the kids loved. The whole ritual of leaving your shoes at the front door and donning slippers, of rolling out the futons at night, of sitting on the floor around a low table for meals, even all leaping into the communal baths was all different and intriguing. The Japanese in the ryokan were very kind to the children and would often pass little gifts of food or drink to them as they left or returned.

We found the Japanese unfailingly interested, helpful and polite. You simply could not look lost for a minute without somebody coming over to offer to help. More than once one of us would be waiting for the other at a train station and it was really necessary to 'look' as if you knew what you were doing or someone or other would come rushing over to offer assistance. Despite the inevitable language difficulties Japan is a surprisingly easy country to get around; everything works so smoothly and clearly that even the mysteries of the Tokyo subway are quickly deciphered with a little help from the colour-coded clues.

Food was easy too; most restaurants display plastic models of what's on offer in windows to the street. You just have to accompany the waiter outside and point out what you want. Of course paying for it is not quite so easy, and has got decidedly worse since our visit, but there are many ways around the high cost of living in Japan. In Kyoto, for example, we would make up a breakfast of rolls from a bakery, fruit, yoghurt and juice from a supermarket and then eat it in the beautiful gardens of a nearby temple. (I must admit that once in Tokyo, however, we resorted to McDonalds!)

Hong Kong and Macau were equally successful. The sheer frenetic pace of Hong Kong keeps everybody on their toes but there is plenty to appeal to children from strolls around the peak, rides on the Star Ferry or a visit to the wonderful Ocean Park. Even business can continue with children; at a dinner with a business acquaintance he brought his children along as well and the four of them were enthralled by a wonderful noodle spinning display right in the middle of the restaurant.

Macau, I must admit, we were glad to get out of – wonderful city though it is. There haven't been many places where we've been holed up in our hotel for a couple of days, experiencing a near miss from a cyclone!

Tony Wheeler

JAPAN

Travelling in Japan with a baby or child is pretty easy; quite possibly the least problematic of all Asian countries for travelling parents. Japan is child-oriented and provides a good standard of sanitation, hygiene and child-care facilities. A good example of the Japanese attitude to children is the fact that adults will give up their seats on trains and buses to children.

Whilst discreet breast-feeding and nappy changing in public are quite acceptable, department stores in Tokyo and other cities have 'mothers' rooms where you can feed and change your child in peace and comfort. These rooms are generally well equipped with cots, changing tables, chairs, boiling water for mixing formulas, sinks with hot and cold water and sometimes even a weighing machine and height/length measurer! They are situated in the baby/child products area which are well stocked with clothes, cloth and disposable nappies. There are also all types of baby equipment such as cots, buggies, bottles etc, plus tinned, bottled and dried foods and drink. These things can also be purchased in most large supermarkets and some chemists, which are generally the cheapest.

The Japanese greeted us warmly wherever we went and were all very interested in the *gaijin aka-chan* – the foreign baby – and were most keen to cuddle and play with him. Luckily Thomas has always been a very sociable baby or this could have been a big problem. One thing I found hard to cope with was the unsolicited advice I'd receive from older Japanese women while out with Thomas, generally along the lines of 'don't you think he's too hot/cold/hungry/thirsty/tired'. I would smile politely through gritted teeth; they only meant well but I did wish they would mind their own business!

In Japan hospitals can be used in the same way that we use a general practitioner and the medical attention I received there was good but expensive. Should you need medical attention in Tokyo the best idea is to ring the tourist office (TIC) for the phone number of the nearest hospital and then telephone the hospital to see if there are any English speaking staff. Alternatively the TIC's free newspaper for tourists, *The Tour Companion*, lists a few hospitals and dentists catering for foreigners as does the *Tokyo Journal* which is available at hotels and English language book shops, however, these publications only cover Tokyo.

We toured Japan from Yoron, a coral island just south of Okinawa, through Honshu to Hokkaido, while Thomas was three and four months old, staying at *minshukus* (you have a room in the house of a Japanese family) and camping sites. Minshukus are great for babies as the rooms have only a *tatami* (straw) mat floor (mattresses which are stored away in a cupboard during the day) and sometimes a small table and TV. With the mattresses going straight onto the tatami no cot (crib) was necessary.

Meal times could be a bit difficult as minshukus rarely supply high chairs (although Thomas was too small for one anyway). However, we found that there was always a member of the minshuku family who was only too willing to cuddle him while we ate. This also used to happen in restaurants. We usually chose traditional style restaurants where we could lie him down on the tatami floor with some toys while we had our meal. Most modern family restaurants have high chairs.

Campsites in Japan tend to be rather basic with non-flush toilets and cold running water, but this is no problem in a country where *sento* (public baths) are so popular. They are very cheap and are usually situated in the older part of town. The changing area often has a tatami floor and occasionally a changing table but once in the bathing area it can be a little tricky, if alone, to have a good wash while clutching a slippery, wriggling baby, too small to sit alone. Again, I found that there were always plenty of fellow bathers only too willing to lend a capable hand. For washing clothes whilst on the move, we used coin laundries.

Since he was so small we carried Thomas around in a sling, but for older children I would think that a buggy is really necessary although it would have to a very lightweight folding one to cope with the buses, trains and many flights of stairs at the stations.

While Japan does not require foreign visitors to have any specific vaccinations I think it is important to know that all babies born in Japan are given a BCG at four months of age as TB is still a problem there. I really feel that children visiting Japan should first have a BCG.

Lynne Mitchell

CHINA

In strong contrast to Japan which we visited about the same time I found it very difficult to tour China with a baby and I really would have enjoyed the trip much more if Thomas had not been with us. This was mainly due to my lack of confidence in the country's medical facilities; I was paranoid that we were going to fall ill.

We also made the great mistake of being there in July when temperatures were generally over 40°C and humidity was very high. I was constantly concerned that Thomas was going to dehydrate and get sunstroke and/or sunburn, but he suffered nothing worse than a heavy cold which, apparently, is inevitable in China. Ben and I both caught heavy colds and suffered the mandatory few days of stomach upsets.

Luckily, being only five months, Thomas was still relying on breast milk for most of his diet so his stomach never had to cope with the food which was usually of poor quality and very greasy. We did take a few jars of baby food but had made the mistake of planning to buy all our baby requirements in Hong Kong rather than Japan. In Japan there is a large selection of dried foods and drinks which would have been perfect as the packages are fairly small and light weight. Unfortunately the only dried food we could find in Hong Kong were very large tins of rice cereal so we had to buy jars instead. We had no problem in purchasing 300 disposable nappies which lasted us the 3½ weeks of the trip. These things are not available at all in China, although I understand that Heinz is opening a baby food factory in Canton for the Chinese market but I don't know when this will be in operation.

In China only very young children wear nappies which are actually just a piece of rectangular cloth held in place by string tied around the baby's middle. As they get older babies have slits in their trousers through which they perform their bodily functions no matter where they are. I got the impression that the Chinese thought Thomas' nappies were rather barbaric! We met a Belgian couple in Beijing who were travelling with their year old son and three year old daughter. They had chosen to bring a few cloth nappies rather than disposables, to cut down on baggage, but it meant that they had to wash them every night. We found that our bag of nappies was very light although maybe rather bulky and as our supply diminished we had room for all our purchases.

We also took a Camping Gaz stove which would probably seem a rather unnecessary piece of luggage to most, but we used it daily to stew fruit for Thomas once we had used all the baby food. There is always a good supply of piping-hot boiled water in flasks at hotels and on trains, and some hotels also provide a carafe of cooled boiled water for immediate consumption. One fellow traveller complained to me that having telephoned room service for more water they waited hours for it to arrive – we found that if we walked down to the attendant's desk, which is situated on each floor of a hotel, flask in hand, we got our water immediately. For sterilising Thomas' bottles we had a plastic kitchen container which was packed full of stuff while on the move, and at night sterilised everything with water from the flask and a drop of sterilising fluid.

Travelling China with a baby was expensive as we felt it was necessary to have our own room and bathroom rather than sharing a dormitory. None of the hotels ever had a cot so we either pushed the twin beds together to fit the three of us, or made a nest for Thomas on the floor if there were suitable cushions and the floor was clean enough. The standard of cleanliness in hotels was usually rather poor, especially considering the highly inflated prices foreigners are made to pay.

We took a ship from Hong Kong to Shanghai and for our first night in China decided to break ourselves in slowly by staying at the *Peace Hotel* which, the hotel receptionist proudly informed us, was one of the best hotels in China. Our first room had no lighting whatsoever and on request we were immediately moved to another room. This, although lit, was filthy with dirty sheets, nut shells on the carpet and a grimy line around the bath. The three of us awoke next morning covered in bed bug bites, but I have to say that on complaining to the manager 50% of our bill was deducted. Maybe we were expecting too much, but we did think we were entitled to western standards if we were paying western prices. Most of the hotels were OK although we did get into the habit of asking to see the room before agreeing to take it, so that we could point out the dirty sheets and the broken toilet! The hotel staff were always happy to do this.

On trains the soft class prices are roughly equivalent to plane fares so we stuck to hard class which was fine. Again we were slowed down by Thomas as we didn't feel we could take him on long journeys in 3rd class, which only supply hard bench seats, so we often had to wait a day or two longer to get hard class tickets. It wasn't always possible to book a bottom bunk although the China International Travel Service Staff at hotels always tried to do this for us. We found that our fellow passengers were always willing to swap over so that Thomas and I could have a bottom bunk, where he slept down one end with me up the other with my legs and feet stopping him from rolling off – not vastly comfortable but good enough. One problem was that the train would give a loud whistle at every station visited through the night which never failed to awaken Thomas and consequently nearly everyone else in our carriage. It's a good job the Chinese love children so much!

The Chinese we met on the trains were marvellous and did their utmost to make us feel comfortable and welcome, offering us food and drink, and spending hours keeping Thomas amused on those long journeys. I think I can safely say that the food served on the trains was the worst in the country

– even the Chinese passengers told us it tasted bad. Whenever we stopped at stations we joined the rest of the train's population on the platform trying to buy fruit, bread, cake and drinks from the stalls. In the frantic crush of everyone trying to get served in the few minutes the train was stopping at the station I found that the stall keepers would always serve foreigners first which luckily never seemed to upset the Chinese in front of me.

Bus journeys were also rather a treat because of the way the Chinese passengers would look after us. A number of hands would pull us on to the bus and if no-one offered their seat immediately someone would be bullied into doing so by the other passengers – they were always very concerned that Thomas, who travelled in a sling, was safe. Once they had ascertained our destination they would discuss us happily until our stop was imminent when they would bodily help me up, escort us to the door and instruct those waiting to get on (usually in a mad scrum) to stand back and let us off.

Foreigner watching is an extremely popular sport in China – you only have to stop in the street for a minute to be completely surrounded by a large group of openly staring and inquisitive but also friendly and smiling people. Breast feeding seemed to be the only time my privacy was considered and it was no problem to do this outside. However, because of the intense heat I tended to use the foreigners' rooms often found at tourist attractions which supplied refreshments at inflated prices and the bliss of an electric fan. In towns I would go to the nearest foreigners' hotel lobby and breast feed in the luxury of air-conditioning. Soft class waiting rooms at stations were another good retreat as the staff would welcome any foreigner no matter what class of ticket they had. Due to its curiosity value nappy changing in public was a big crowd puller but never upset anyone as it can do in the West, but again I tended to use the above mentioned retreats because of the heat.

Thomas always seemed filthy in China, I suppose because of the humidity, but there was always plenty of hot water for washing in the hotels. Although the hotels usually do offer a laundry service I chose to do my own washing as I had heard that occasionally items of clothing get lost while in the laundry.

As we luckily didn't suffer any serious illness I have no idea what the standard of medical attention is like nor the procedure for seeing a doctor. However I suppose the CITS staff or hotel receptionist would be able to help. China no longer requires vaccinations and malarial protection is not necessary, but like Japan I feel it is very important for children to at least have a BCG.

Lynne Mitchell

CHINA

We were amazed by the warmth and enthusiasm of the Chinese, particularly the grandmothers, towards our family. In China, where there is a one couple-one child policy, children have special status and are treated very well; in fact they celebrate Children's Day on 1 June. On that day my five year old daughter received a 'much coveted' railhead pin from the Emei station master.

Children can travel free on trains until they are one metre high. Between one and 1.3 metres the fare is 25%, after that it's full fare. On buses and boats, however, there was no charge, and no matter how crowded the city buses, someone *always* offered her a seat. Often she sat beside the conductor! The boats, however, offered the best value. On all the boat journeys she enjoyed herself by making friends and having Mandarin lessons.

Hotel accommodation was quite satisfactory. Travelling with a child seems to give you a certain amount of leverage. Boiled water is available everywhere but get some orange flavoured crystals to relieve the monotony. Although our child became adept with chopsticks a fork was usually made available; forks would come from the most peculiar places, as if out of air.

Kids are fickle eaters anywhere, consequently we all ate a lot of sweet 'n sour pork, peanuts and yoghurt. Generally noodle shops offer nothing to drink so bring along the water bottle to fend off a thirst crisis. Stock up on children's aspirin, vitamin C and cough syrup; we could find no satisfactory local substitute.

China has many attractions for children. A trip to the market to buy a fat pig makes their nursery rhymes come alive. Bicycles can be rented in a few places but watch those bamboo front seats – there is no protection for feet which are too easily caught in the spokes. Most cities have zoos and there are parks everywhere, some with swings and slides. We saw a marvellous puppet show in Yangshuo, acrobats in Shanghai and Kunming had plenty of street entertainment — gymnasts, jugglers, salesmen and so on.

Our daughter had little trouble handling stares. There was always a buffer zone around us — a lot of looking, not much touching. By the time we left China she was practising characters, adding with the abacus and speaking Mandarin. She loved being in China and they loved her. In Dali she was the first western pre-schooler to visit and as we walked down the street people came out of their houses with presents for her. They all wanted to meet the 'foreign child'.

Walter & Sunny Cherry

Health

Travel health depends on your pre-departure preparations, your day-to-day health care while travelling and how you handle any medical problem or emergency that does develop. While the list of potential dangers can seem quite frightening, with a little luck, some basic precautions and adequate information few travellers or their children experience more than upset stomachs. Our children have travelled with us in Africa, Australia, New Zealand, the Pacific, numerous places in Asia and in North and South America and, touch wood, never had any health problems.

Travel Health Guides

There are a number of books on travel health:

Staying Healthy in Asia, Africa & Latin America, Volunteers in Asia Press, 1988. This is probably the best all round guide to carry as it's compact but very detailed and well organised. If you just want a handy guide that tells you what to do when you come up against a problem this books is terrific.
Travellers' Health, Dr Richard Dawood, Oxford University Press, 1986. This book is comprehensive, easy to read, authoritative and also highly recommended although it's rather large to lug around. If you want to know the full story behind any potential medical problem and detailed coverage on what to do then this book is excellent.

Pre-Departure Preparations

Health Insurance A travel insurance policy to cover theft, loss and medical problems is a wise idea. There are a wide variety of policies and your travel agent will have recommendations. The international student travel policies handled by STA Travel or other student travel organisations are usually good value. Some policies offer lower and higher medical expenses options but the higher one is chiefly for countries like the US with extremely high medical costs. Check the small print:

Some policies specifically exclude 'dangerous activities' which can even include activities like trekking. If doing something 'dangerous' is on your agenda you don't want that sort of policy.

You may prefer a policy which pays doctors or hospitals direct rather than you having to pay now and claim later. If you have to claim later make sure you keep all documentation. Some policies ask you to call back (reverse charges) to a centre in your home country where an immediate assessment of your problem is made.

Check if the policy covers ambulances or an emergency flight home. If you have to stretch out you will need two seats and somebody has to pay for it!

Medical Kit A small, straightforward medical kit put together with special thought for children's ailments is a wise thing to carry. In many countries if a medicine is available at all it will generally be available over the counter and the price will be much cheaper than in the West. A possible kit list includes:

Infant analgesic – with measuring cup or dropper.

Antihistamine (such as Benadryl) – useful as a decongestant for colds, allergies, to ease the itch from insect bites or stings or to help prevent motion sickness.

Antibiotics – useful if you're travelling well off the beaten track, but it must be prescribed and you should carry the prescription with you.

Kaolin preparation (Pepto-Bismol), Imodium – for stomach upsets.

Rehydration mixture – for treatment of severe diarrhoea. This is particularly important if travelling with children. An electrolyte mixture is available in sachets.

Antiseptic (like Dettol), mercurochrome and antibiotic powder or similar 'dry' spray – for cuts and grazes.

Calamine lotion – to ease irritation from sunburn, bites or stings.

Bandages, band-aids, gauze and cotton wool – for minor injuries.

Scissors, tweezers and a thermometer/ fever strips – mercury thermometers are prohibited by airlines.

Insect repellent (check that it is suitable for children's skin), sun blocker, suntan lotion, chap stick and water purification tablets.

If your child is still very young bring cream for nappy rash; if teething bring teething gel.

Worm treatment, lice shampoo and perhaps an anti-fungal powder.

Ideally antibiotics should be administered only under medical supervision and should never be taken indiscriminately. Over use of antibiotics can weaken your child's ability to deal with infections naturally and can reduce the drug's efficacy on a future occasion. Administer only the recommended dose at the prescribed intervals and continue using the antibiotic for the prescribed period, even if the illness seems to be cured earlier. Antibiotics are quite specific to the infections they can treat. If you are unsure you have the correct one, don't use it and stop immediately if there are any serious reactions such as a skin rash, itching or difficulty in breathing.

Be careful of buying drugs in developing countries, particularly where the expiry date may have passed or correct storage conditions not followed. In many Third World countries drugs may be dispensed which are no longer recommended, or have even been banned in the west.

Health Preparations Make sure your children are healthy before you start travelling. If they wear glasses take a spare pair and their prescription. If they take any medication take an adequate supply as it may not be available locally. Take the prescription, with the generic rather than the brand name (which may not be locally available), as it will make getting replacements easier. It's a wise idea to have the prescription with you to show you legally use the medication; it's surprising how often over-the-counter drugs from one place are illegal without a prescription or even banned in another.

Immunisations Vaccinations provide protection against diseases you might meet along the way. For some countries no immunisations are necessary but the further off the beaten track you go the more necessary it is to take precautions. These days vaccination as an entry requirement is usually only enforced when you are coming from an infected area – yellow fever and cholera are the two most likely requirements. Nevertheless, all vaccinations should be recorded on an International Health Certificate which is available from your physician or health department.

Plan ahead for getting vaccinations since some of them require an initial shot followed by a booster while some vaccinations should not be given together. Most children in the West will have been immunised against various diseases during their first few years but your doctor may still recommend booster shots against measles or polio, diseases still prevalent in many developing countries. Apart from these, special vaccinations for travelling are not normally given to children under 12 months of age. Regardless of how you feel about inoculations, if you plan to take your children travelling you are placing them at some risk. In some parts of the world the infant mortality rate is horrendous and diseases which are no longer a problem in the West, due to widespread vaccination programmes, are still very serious health risks.

There are two kinds of vaccine, live and killed. A live vaccine is an actual organism that can multiply and grow but does not cause disease in humans. The human body produces antibodies in reaction to these organisms, making the vaccinated person immune. Immunity gained in this way is long lived and may even be permanent. This type of vaccination is generally contraindicated if you are pregnant or are likely to become pregnant within three months of the vaccination.

A killed vaccine is not infectious. It poses no danger to pregnant women unless it is likely to cause a very high temperature. The body produces antibodies to a killed vaccine to produce an immunity to the disease. This immunity is not permanent so periodic booster shots are required.

In some countries immunisations are available from airport or government health centres, and in some countries you wouldn't want to be injected! Travel agents or airline offices will tell you where. The possible list of vaccinations includes:

Smallpox Smallpox has now been wiped out worldwide so immunisation is no longer necessary.
Cholera Some countries may require cholera vaccination if you are coming from an infected area but protection is not very effective, and only lasts six months. This is a killed vaccine which is contraindicated for pregnancy. Cholera protection is given to children over 12 months old.
Tetanus & Diphtheria Boosters are necessary every 10 years and protection is highly recommended. While this is not an entry requirement for any country, it

is a very sensible precaution to take, especially for children who often suffer minor cuts.

Typhoid Protection lasts for three years and is useful if you are travelling for long periods in rural, tropical areas. You may get some side effects such as pain at the injection site, fever, headache and a general unwell feeling. The vaccination is a killed bacterial vaccine and is given to children over two years old. Typhoid immunisation requires two doses and is not considered safe during pregnancy.

Infectious Hepatitis Gamma globulin is not a vaccination but a ready-made antibody which has proven very successful in reducing the chances of hepatitis infection. Because it may interfere with the development of immunity, it should not be given until at least 10 days after administration of the last vaccine needed and as close as possible to departure because of its relatively short-lived protection period of six months. Hepatitis protection is not an entry requirement anywhere and the injection is given intramuscularly.

Yellow Fever Protection lasts 10 years and is recommended where the disease is endemic, chiefly in Africa and Latin America within 15° either side of the equator. You usually have to go to a special yellow fever vaccination centre for this live vaccine. This vaccination is contraindicated in pregnancy. If you possibly can you should avoid yellow fever areas when you are pregnant.

Meningitis This vaccination is recommended for people trekking in Nepal and for visitors to some areas of Africa and Brazil. It is given as a single injection and gives immunity for up to three years duration.

Basic Rules

Care in what you eat and drink is the most important health rule. Stomach upsets are the most likely travel health problem but the majority of these upsets will be relatively minor. Don't become paranoid; trying the local food is part of the experience of travel after all.

The number one rule is *don't drink the water* and that includes ice. If you don't know for certain that water is safe always assume the worst. Reputable brands of bottled water or soft drinks are generally fine although in some places refilled bottles are not unknown. Beware of street vendors selling brand name drinks in very battered looking bottles, with rusty caps and each bottle filled to a different level. Take care with fruit juice, particularly if water may have been added. Milk should be treated with suspicion as it is often unpasteurised. Boiled milk is fine if it is kept hygienically and yoghurt is always good.

Salads and fruit should be washed with purified water or peeled where possible. Ice cream is usually OK if it is a reputable brand name but beware of Third World street vendors selling ice cream that has melted and been refrozen. Thoroughly cooked food is safest but not if it has been left to cool or if it has been reheated. Take great care with shellfish or fish and avoid under cooked meat. If a place looks clean and well run and the vendor also looks clean and healthy then the food is probably safe. In general places that are packed with travellers or locals will be fine, empty restaurants are questionable.

In summary the basic rules for general health in Third World countries are:

Make sure your children's hands are clean; carry wet wipes everywhere.
Clean teeth and wash toothbrushes with boiled or purified water.
Don't let them eat raw fruit or vegetables unless you know they have been thoroughly washed in purified water or you have peeled the fruit.
Avoid water and ice unless you are certain it has been boiled or purified. Assume that all water or fresh food that has been washed in water is unsafe unless you positively know otherwise.
For small children try to regularly sterilise utensils they use. Soaking them in boiled or purified water with a sterilising tab will do. An empty 'baby wipe' container, a plastic ice cream container or a large Tupperware will make a fine sterilising unit.

Nutrition If the food you find is poor or limited in availability, if meals are missed or if your children simply loose their appetite their health can soon be at risk. Make sure you all have a balanced diet. Eggs, tofu, beans, lentils (*dhal* in India) and nuts are all safe ways to get protein. Fruit you can peel (bananas, oranges or mandarins for example) are always safe and a good source of vitamins. Make sure they get plenty of grains (rice) and bread. Remember that although food is generally safer if it is cooked well, over cooked food loses much of its nutritional value. If the food is insufficient it's a good idea to take vitamin and iron pills.

In hot climates make sure your children drink enough; don't rely on them feeling thirsty to indicate they should drink. If you are breast feeding be prepared to feed much more frequently, or remember to give frequent drinks from a bottle. Not needing to urinate or very dark yellow urine is a danger sign. Another simple test is to pinch a small portion of the skin on the soft part of the forearm. Hold it up for a second, then let it go. If the skin goes back slowly rather than immediately plopping back, your child may be dehydrated.

Always carry a water bottle with you and give frequent drinks. Excessive sweating can lead to loss of salt and therefore muscle cramping. Salt tablets are not a good idea as a preventative but in places where salt is not used much, adding additional salt to food can help.

Water Purification The simplest way of purifying water is to thoroughly boil it. Technically this means for 10 minutes, something which happens very rarely! Remember that at high altitude water boils at a lower temperature so germs are less likely to be killed. Once purified, water should be stored in a sterilised container or you risk recontaminating it.

Simple filtering will not remove all dangerous organisms so if you cannot boil water it should be treated chemically. Chlorine tablets (puritabs, steritabs or other brand names) will kill many but not all pathogens. They will not kill amoebic cysts. Iodine is very effective in purifying water and is available in tablet form (such as Potable Aqua) but follow the directions carefully and remember that too much iodine can be harmful.

If you can't find tablets, tincture of iodine (2%) or iodine crystals can be used. Two drops of tincture of iodine per litre or quart of clear water is the recommended dosage which should then be left to stand for 30 minutes. Iodine crystals can also be used to purify water but this is a more complicated process as you have to first prepare a saturated iodine solution. Iodine loses its effectiveness if exposed to air or damp so keep it in a tightly sealed container.

To use iodine crystals take a small bottle (25 to 30 ml) and put four to eight grams of *resublimed iodine* in it. This should be available from your pharmacist. Fill the bottle with water and shake it vigorously for 30 to 60 seconds to make a saturated solution. Not all the iodine will dissolve, crystals will remain in the saturated solution.

To purify water first hold the solution upright for a few moments so that the iodine crystals fall to the bottom. Then add 12.5 ml (about half the bottle, make a measuring mark for accuracy) of this saturated water-iodine solution to one litre of water. Leave to stand for 15 minutes, or up to 40 minutes if the water is cloudy. The water is then safe to drink.

The same crystals can be used almost 1000 times. You just refill the bottle each time to make a new lot of the saturated solution. You must be very careful not to allow the crystals to 'escape' into your drinking water, it may be a good idea to fix a piece of muslin or mesh over the top of the bottle. Iodine is poisonous if taken in quantity and one crystal may rate as quantity, especially for children.

If you suffer from a thyroid complaint, consult your doctor before using any method involving iodine. Don't use it continuously; where possible boil water instead and save the iodine-treated water for the occasion when you really need it. Keep the bottle with the iodine crystals filled with water, even when not in use, otherwise you may find the vapour will penetrate the cap and cause havoc wherever it is packed.

I usually take flavoured powder to dissolve in the water, it disguises the taste of the iodine and the children think they are having a soft drink instead of just water.

Health A normal body temperature is 37°C, more than 2°C higher is a 'high' fever. A normal adult pulse rate is 60 to 80 per minute, children 80 to 100, babies 100 to 140. You should know how to take a temperature and a pulse rate. As a general rule the pulse increases about 20 beats per minute for each °C rise in fever.

Respiration rate (breathing) is also an indicator of illness. Count the number of breaths per minute; between 12 and 20 is normal for adults and older children, up to 30 for younger children, and 40 for babies. People with a high fever or serious respiratory illness (like pneumonia) breathe more quickly than normal. As a rule of thumb more than 40 shallow breaths a minute usually means pneumonia.

Many health problems can be avoided by simply taking care. Make sure your children wash their hands frequently; it's quite easy to contaminate your own food. Make sure they clean their teeth with purified water rather than straight from the tap. Avoid climatic extremes; keep them out of the sun when it's hot and dress them warmly when it's cold. Avoid potential diseases by making sure they dress sensibly. They can get worm infections through bare feet or dangerous coral cuts by walking over coral without shoes.

Avoid insect bites by covering bare skin when insects are around, by screening windows or beds and by using insect repellents. Seek local advice; if you're told the water is unsafe due to jellyfish, crocodiles or bilharzia, don't go in. In situations were there is no information, discretion is the better part of valour.

Medical Problems & Treatment

Potential medical problems can be broken down into several areas. First there are the climatic and geographical considerations – problems caused by extremes of temperature, altitude or motion. Then there are diseases and illnesses caused by insanitation, insect bites or stings, animal or human contact. Simple cuts, bites or scratches can also cause problems.

Self diagnosis and treatment can be risky; wherever possible seek qualified help, although in some places the standards of medical attention are so low that for some ailments the best advice is to get on a plane and go somewhere else. If you need to find a doctor there are several places you can try:

Your hotel, or any expensive hotel in the area, should be able to give you the name and address of a doctor, although it's possible that expensive hotels will recommend equally expensive doctors.

An embassy – either yours or some other embassy for a western country may have a list of medical practitioners that their staff use. In some countries treatment at regular public hospitals can be surprisingly good.

The International Association for Medical Assistance to Travelers (IAMAT) is a non-profit organisation which exists on donations. They will give you a directory of English-speaking physicians abroad whom the organisation considers trained to western medical standards. The doctors involved also agree to abide by a schedule of payments set by IAMAT. They produce a booklet (available for a donation of US$25 or more) which gives information on climate conditions, suggestions for proper clothing and descriptions of sanitary conditions of water, milk and food in 1440 major cities around the world. Their address is IAMAT, Suite 5620, 350 Fifth Ave, New York, NY 10001, USA.

Another organisation is Intermedic, which provides a list of English-speaking doctors in 200 cities who have all agreed to a set fee schedule. They also give information on immunisations and medications needed for any trip. A family membership of US$10 is charged. Their address is Intermedic, 777 Third Ave, New York, NY 10017, USA.

Some travel insurance policies maintain lists of practitioners in countries throughout the world. When you need assistance you phone back home, reverse charges, and they tell you who to get in touch with, or even arrange for the local doctor to see you.

Fever

Children often have high fevers for little apparent reason and recover from them remarkably quickly. Carry a thermometer and, if your children are very young, fever strips (those little strips which will tell you immediately if your child does have a fever). I find it easier to use these in the first instance as most small children are not too cooperative when having to sit still with a thermometer in their mouths for the required time. If the strip does indicate fever, use the thermometer to find out just how hot your child is. As you would normally do, try to get medical help if the temperature is abnormally high. Fevers in small children can be quite dangerous.

The general rule with treating fevers is to get the child cool as quickly as possible. Remove all clothes, sponge the child down with cool water, place close to a fan, and try to get them to drink something cool. If the temperature is high, place them in a cool bath. The child won't want to go, and may shiver because they are hot, but you must bring the temperature down. Administer paracetamol (eg Panadol).

Children often run temperatures without ill effect; my most frightening experience was in Africa with Kieran. We were all sleeping in a rather small tent whilst a herd of elephants grazed outside. One male elephant in particular was considered more than a bit of a nuisance and was acting quite aggressively towards our camp. Since I found the sound of elephants grazing right by my head rather unsettling to say the least, I was not sleeping very well. In the middle of the night Kieran woke up, delirious and very feverish. Trying to calm him, get his fever down, keep him quiet, so as not to alarm the pachyderms, while remaining calm myself, was not easy. I was sure he had malaria, meningitis, sleeping sickness, etc. Next day, a rather tired but otherwise totally healthy Kieran awoke; I was a complete wreck. Treat fevers seriously, and always call in medical help if you are at all concerned.

Climatic & Geographical Considerations

Sunburn In the tropics, the desert or at high altitude you can get sunburnt surprisingly quickly even through cloud. Use a sunscreen and take extra care to cover areas which don't normally see sun – feet for example. A hat provides added protection and use zinc cream or some other barrier cream for noses and lips. Calamine lotion is good for mild sunburn.

Apart from sunburn, there is evidence that overexposure to the sun can cause skin cancer to start from a very early age even though

its presence may not become noticeable until much, much later. Small children burn easily, so always use sunscreen with babies, even if you are only taking them for a five-minute walk around the corner to get lunch. Remember the sun is at its strongest around noon, but for most of the day in many countries it is strong enough to burn a baby very severely. Early morning and late afternoon are fine times to take the children to the beach; it is usually warm enough to really enjoy the water and the sand, but not hot enough to do any harm. An umbrella may be a good idea to take to the beach to use as a sunshade, especially if you have a small baby who is not yet crawling or walking.

For the first week cover your children with a complete sun block any time they are in the sun, other than for a short while (say 15 minutes) early morning (before 10 am) and late afternoon (after 4 or 5 pm). Even though the sun doesn't feel too hot then, use a sun screen (water-resistant if they will be in the water). A T-shirt or light cotton caftan will also give protection and can be worn in the water. It is possible to burn through the T-shirt, especially when it is wet, so be careful. The danger of sunburn is greater at the beach than anywhere else as the sun reflects off the sand and water.

If your children do get burnt calamine lotion is a good standby, but there are other lotions you can get. Have a pair of sandals or beach shoes on hand as the sand can get hot enough to burn, badly, little, tender-skinned feet.

Try to get your children to wear a hat – both my children when they were very small promptly ripped hats off as soon as I put them on but it is worth persevering.

Prickly Heat Prickly heat is an itchy rash caused by excessive perspiration trapped under the skin. It usually strikes people who have just arrived in a hot climate whose pores have not yet opened sufficiently to cope with greater sweating. Keeping cool will help so make sure your children are dressed in cool cotton clothes. After washing dry your children carefully, especially skin folds. I don't recommend using powder as I think it may block the pores. Cool wash-downs and use of calamine lotion or a similar preparation will help alleviate the problem. Staying in a hotel with air-conditioning will help. If the rash is very bad check with a local pharmacy. If there is a history of hives or other allergic reactions in your family, ask your doctor's advice before you leave. Sometimes an antihistamine cream or medication is useful in severe cases.

Heat Exhaustion If your child complains of aches and pains in the joints, it may be due to heat exhaustion which can be caused by dehydration or salt deficiency. Take time to acclimatise to high temperatures and make sure you get sufficient liquids. Salt deficiency is characterised by fatigue, lethargy, headaches, giddiness and muscle cramps. A little salt added to the food will generally take care of this. It is probably a good idea to try to include some salty foods in your diet, even if you normally don't use salt. Vomiting or diarrhoea can deplete your liquid and salt levels.

Heat Stroke This serious, sometimes fatal, condition can occur if the body's heat regulating mechanism breaks down and the body temperature rises to dangerous levels. Long, continuous periods of exposure to high temperatures can leave you vulnerable to heat stroke.

The symptoms are feeling unwell, not sweating very much or at all, and high body temperature (39 to 41°C). Where sweating has ceased the skin becomes flushed and red. Severe, throbbing headaches and lack of coordination will also occur and the sufferer may be confused or aggressive. Eventually the victim will become delirious or convulse. Hospitalisation is essential but meanwhile get the victim out of the sun, remove clothing, cover him with a wet sheet or towel and then fan continually.

Fungal Infections Hot weather fungal infections are most likely to occur on the scalp, between the toes or fingers (athlete's foot), in the groin and ringworm on the body. You get ringworm (which is a fungus infection, not a worm) from infected animals or by walking on damp areas, like shower floors.

To prevent fungal infections wear loose, comfortable clothes, avoid artificial fibres, wash frequently and dry carefully. If you do get an infection, wash the infected area daily with a disinfectant or medicated soap and water and rinse and dry well. Apply an anti-fungal powder like the widely available Tinaderm. Try to expose the infected area to air or sunlight as much as possible and wash all towels and underwear in hot water and change them often.

Cold Too much cold is just as dangerous as too much heat, particularly if it leads to hypothermia. If you are trekking at high altitudes or simply taking a long bus trip over mountains, particularly at night, be prepared. In some countries (Tibet, Chile) you should always be prepared for cold, wet or windy conditions even if you're just out walking.

Hypothermia occurs when the body loses heat faster than it can produce it and the core temperature of the body falls. It is surprisingly easy to progress from very cold to dangerously cold due to a combination of wind, wet clothing, fatigue and hunger, even if the air temperature is above freezing. It is best to dress in layers; silk, wool and some of the new artificial fibres are all good insulating materials. A hat is important as a lot of heat is lost through the head. A strong, waterproof outer layer is essential as keeping dry is vital. Carry basic supplies, including food containing simple sugars to generate heat quickly, and lots of fluid to drink.

Symptoms of hypothermia are exhaustion, numb skin (particularly toes and fingers), shivering, slurred speech, irrational or violent behaviour, lethargy, stumbling, dizzy spells, muscle cramps and violent bursts of energy. Irrationality may take the form of sufferers claiming they are warm and trying to take off their clothes.

To treat hypothermia first get out of the wind and/or rain, remove wet clothing and replace with dry, warm clothing. Drink hot liquids, not alcohol, and eat some high calorie, easily digestible food. This should be enough for the early stages of hypothermia but if it has gone further it may be necessary to place the victim in a warm sleeping bag and get in with them. Do not rub the patient, place them near a fire or remove wet clothes in the wind. If possible place in a warm (not hot) bath.

Children are more susceptible to changes of temperature and lose body heat faster than adults, if you are taking them to areas where such rapid temperature changes can occur, make sure you know what you are doing and are completely prepared.

Altitude Sickness Acute Mountain Sickness or AMS occurs at high altitude and can be fatal. The lack of oxygen at high altitudes affects most people to some extent. Take it easy at first, increase liquid intake and eat well. Even with acclimatisation you may still have trouble adjusting – headaches, nausea, dizziness, a dry cough, insomnia, breathlessness, loss of appetite are all signs to heed. If you reach a high altitude by trekking, acclimatisation takes place gradually and you are less likely to be affected than if you fly straight there.

Mild altitude problems will generally abate after a day or so but if the symptoms persist or become worse the only treatment is to descend, even 500 metres can help. Breathlessness, a dry, irritative cough (which may progress to the production of pink, frothy sputum), severe headache, loss of appetite, nausea, and vomiting are all danger signs. Increasing tiredness, confusion and lack of coordination and balance are real danger signs. Any of these symptoms individually, even just a persistent headache, can be a warning.

There is no hard and fast rule as to how high is too high, AMS has been fatal at altitudes of 3000 metres, although 3500 to 4500 metres is the usual range. It is wise to always sleep at a lower altitude than the greatest height reached during the day.

Again this is an illness which will affect children more quickly and seriously than adults.

Motion Sickness Eating lightly before and during a trip will reduce the chances of motion sickness. If your children are prone to motion sickness try to find a place that minimises disturbance – near the wing on aircraft, close to midships on boats, near the centre on buses. Fresh air usually helps, reading or cigarette smoke doesn't. Commercial preparations to prevent motion sickness can cause drowsiness and have to be taken before the trip commences; when they're feeling sick it's too late. Ginger is a natural preventative and is available in capsule form.

Diseases of Insanitation

Diarrhoea A change of water, food or climate can all cause the runs, but more serious is diarrhoea due to contaminated food or water. Totally breast fed babies are normally safe but despite all your precautions older children may still have a bout of mild travellers' diarrhoea. A few rushed toilet trips with no other symptoms is not indicative of a serious problem. Moderate diarrhoea, involving half a dozen loose movements in a day, is more of a nuisance.

With small children there is not much you can do; most doctors do not recommend giving any specific medication, just lots of rest and plenty to drink. Don't try to coax them to eat; if they feel like it they will, otherwise they'll make up for fasting when they are well again. Dairy products should be avoided because they 'feed the bugs', not the child, and will only exacerbate the condition. Flat lemonade, Coke or other soft drinks diluted with water (50:50) and soda water are all recommended. A bland diet is recommended until they recover.

Dehydration is the main danger with any diarrhoea, particularly for children who can become weak very quickly, so fluid replenishment is the number one treatment. With severe diarrhoea a rehydrating solution is necessary to keep fluid levels, minerals and salts up. An electrolyte preparation will replace the electrolytes lost to the body and these are available in powder form in sachets or as a tinned ready-mixed variety. The problem with the sachets is that they have to be mixed with water but your doctor should be able to tell you which is the best for your needs.

There are also recipes available for do-it-yourself preparations including this one from *Staying Healthy in Asia, Africa & Latin America*:

One litre of boiled water and half a cup of orange juice or a little lemon juice
Two tablespoons of sugar or honey – honey is best if available
Quarter teaspoon of salt
Quarter teaspoon of baking soda (if you don't have soda use another quarter teaspoonful of salt)

An adult with diarrhoea should drink three or more litres a day, small children at least one litre a day. Adults or children with diarrhoea should drink two glasses after every trip to the bathroom. If vomiting and unable to keep large amounts of liquid down, administer small sips every five minutes.

Lomotil or Imodium can be used to bring relief from the symptoms although they do not actually cure it. For children Imodium is preferable, but do not use these drugs if they have a high fever or are severely dehydrated or have blood, pus or mucus in the stools. If cramping and diarrhoea persist for more than 24 hours after commencing the medication, it should be discontinued and medical help sought.

If the diarrhoea persists for more than a couple of days, if there is blood or mucus in the movements or if the child has a fever then medical help should be sought immediately. If the child seems well and there is no blood or mucus present but the diarrhoea continues, it may well be food poisoning. If this is not severe (I emphasise that the child appears well, is lively and seems bright and healthy), there is not much you can do but wait for the diarrhoea to stop.

Don't feed the child too much, cut out dairy products, give only bland, non-fibrous food and ensure that fluid intake is kept up, and hope it ends soon. Even if there is nothing the doctor can do, I would still seek medical advice. Antibiotics such as ampicillin (not to be taken by anyone allergic to penicillin) can be very useful in treating severe diarrhoea, especially if it is accompanied by nausea, vomiting, stomach cramps or mild fever. Three days treatment should be sufficient and an improvement should occur within 24 hours. You should ask your doctor to recommend a suitable antibiotic and the dosage for such a situation. Carry the prescription with you.

Giardia This intestinal parasite is present in contaminated water and the symptoms are stomach cramps, nausea, bloated stomach, watery, foul-smelling diarrhoea and frequent gas. Giardia can appear several weeks after you have been exposed to the parasite. The symptoms may disappear for a few days and then return; this can go on for several weeks. Metronidazole (known as Flagyl) is the recommended drug but should only be taken under medical supervision. Antibiotics are no use.

Dysentery This serious illness is caused by contaminated food or water and is characterised by severe diarrhoea, often with blood or mucus in the stool. There are two kinds of dysentery. Bacillary dysentery is characterised by a high fever and rapid development. Headache, vomiting and stomach pains are also symptoms. It generally does not last longer than a week, but it is highly contagious.

Amoebic dysentery is more gradual in developing, has no fever or vomiting but is a more serious illness. It is not a self-limiting disease but will persist until treated and can recur and cause long term damage.

A stool test is necessary with dysentery but if no medical care is available tetracycline is the prescribed treatment for bacillary dysentery, and metronidazole for amoebic dysentery.

Tetracycline should not be taken by pregnant women after the fourth month. Children under six years old should only take tetracycline when absolutely necessary and for a short period of time. You must be careful not to use tetracycline that is old or has passed its expiry date.

Cholera Cholera vaccination is not very effective but outbreaks of cholera are generally widely reported so you can avoid such areas. The disease is characterised by a sudden onset of acute diarrhoea with 'rice water' stools, vomiting, muscular cramps, and extreme weakness. You need medical help, but treat for dehydration which can be extreme and if there is an appreciable delay in getting to hospital begin taking tetracycline.

Viral Gastroenteritis This is not caused by bacteria but, as the name suggests, a virus. It is characterised by stomach cramps, diarrhoea and sometimes by vomiting and/or a slight fever. All you can do is rest and drink lots of fluids.

Hepatitis Hepatitis A is the most common form of this disease and is spread by contaminated food or water. The symptoms are fever, chills, headache, fatigue, feelings of weakness and aches and pains. This is followed by loss of appetite, nausea, vomiting, abdominal pain, dark urine, light coloured faeces and jaundiced skin; the whites of the eyes may turn yellow. In some case there may just be a feeling of being unwell or tired, loss of appetite, aches and pains and the jaundiced effect. You should seek medical advice, but in general there is not much you can do apart from rest, drink lots of fluids, eat lightly and avoid fatty foods.

Hepatitis B, which used to be called serum hepatitis, is not a real risk for children. If your child needs to be given an injection and you are dubious about the sanitary conditions in which it must be given, buy a new, sealed syringe from the pharmacy and give it to the doctor. It is better to avoid such situations occurring. Don't have your daughters' ears pierced in developing countries!

Typhoid Typhoid fever is another gut infection that travels the faecal-oral route; ie, contaminated water and food are responsible. Vaccination against typhoid is not totally effective and it is one of the most dangerous infections, so medical help must be sought.

In the early stages, typhoid is like so many other illnesses: your child may appear to have a bad cold or flu on the way as the symptoms are headache, sore throat, and a fever which rises a little each day until it is around 40°C or more. Pulse is often slow for the amount of fever present and gets slower as the fever rises, unlike a normal fever where the pulse increases. There may also be vomiting, diarrhoea or constipation.

In the second week the high fever and slow pulse continue and a few pink spots may appear on the body. There may also be trembling, delirium, weakness, weight loss and dehydration. If there are no further complications, the fever and symptoms will slowly go during the third week. However you must get medical help before this as common complications are pneumonia (acute infection of the lungs) or peritonitis (burst appendix) and typhoid is very infectious.

Treat the fever by keeping them cool and watch for dehydration. Chloramphenicol is the recommended antibiotic, but there are fewer side affects with ampicillin.

Worms These parasites are most common in rural, tropical areas and a stool test when you return home is not a bad idea. They can be present on unwashed vegetables or in under cooked meat and can be picked up through the skin by walking in bare feet. Infestations may not show up for some time, and although they are generally not serious, if left untreated they can cause severe health problems. A stool test is necessary to pinpoint the problem and medication is often available over the counter. Children often get worms, even in the West, so it may be a good idea to carry some worm treatment and pay attention if your children complain of an 'itchy bottom', are very restless while sleeping, wake up often, or go off their food. Talk to your doctor about it before you go.

Diseases Spread by People & Animals
Tetanus This potentially fatal disease is found in undeveloped tropical areas and is difficult to treat but is preventable with immunisation. Tetanus occurs when a wound becomes infected by a germ which lives in the faeces of animals or people, so beware of cuts, punctures or animal bites. Tetanus is known as lockjaw and the first symptoms may be discomfort in swallowing, stiffening of the jaw and neck, followed by painful convulsions of the jaw and whole body.

Rabies Rabies is found in many countries and is caused by a bite or scratch by an infected animal. Dogs are a noted carrier. Any bite, scratch or even lick from a mammal should be cleaned immediately and thoroughly. Scrub with soap and running water, then clean with an alcohol solution. If there is any possibility that the animal is infected medical help should be sought immediately. Even if the animal is not rabid, all bites should be treated seriously as they can become infected or can result in tetanus. A rabies vaccination is now available but is only recommended for people in high risk situations. Fortunately treatment for suspected rabies is no longer as complicated as it once was.

The best solution to this problem is simple prevention. In developing countries animals are rarely cared for like they are in the West and can carry many undesirable germs. Make it clear to your children that animals are to be left alone.

Meningococcal Meningitis Sub-Saharan Africa is considered the 'meningitis belt' and the meningitis season falls at the time most people would be attempting the overland trip across the Sahara – the northern winter before rains come. Other countries which have recurring epidemics are Mongolia, Vietnam, Brazil, the Nile Valley and Nepal.

Trekkers to rural areas of Nepal should be particularly careful as the disease is spread by close contact with people who carry it in their throats and noses, spread it through coughs and sneezes and may not be aware that they are carriers. Lodges in the hills where travellers spend the night are prime spots for the spread of infection.

This very serious disease attacks the brain and can be fatal. A scattered blotchy rash, fever, severe headache, sensitivity to light and neck stiffness which prevents forward bending of the head are the first symptoms. Death can occur within a few hours, so immediate treatment is important.

Treatment is large doses of penicillin given intravenously, or, if that is not possible, intramuscularly (ie, in the buttocks). Vaccination offers good protection for over one year but you should also check for reports of current epidemics. In Kathmandu you can get the vaccination from the International Clinic (tel 410893) in Balawatar, across from the north end of the Soviet Embassy.

Tuberculosis Although this disease is widespread in many undeveloped countries it is not a serious risk to travellers. Young children are more susceptible than adults and vaccination is a sensible precaution for children under 12 travelling in endemic areas. TB is commonly spread by coughing or by unpasteurised dairy products from infected cows. Milk that has been boiled is safe to drink and the souring of milk to make yoghurt or cheese kills the bacilli.

Bilharzia Bilharzia is found in fresh water and is carried by worms which attach themselves to the intestines or the urinary bladder where they produce large numbers of eggs. They enter through the skin and the first indication is a tingling and sometimes a light rash around the area where the worm entered. Weeks later, when the worm is busy producing eggs, a high fever may develop. A general feeling of being unwell may be the first indication, but once the disease is established abdominal pain and blood in the urine are other signs.

The main method of preventing the disease is by avoiding swimming or bathing in fresh water where bilharzia is present. Even deep water can be infected and if your children do get wet, dry them off quickly and dry their clothes as well. Seek medical attention if you have been exposed and tell the doctor your suspicions as bilharzia in the early stages can be confused with malaria or typhoid. If you cannot get medical help immediately Niridazole is the recommended treatment.

Diphtheria Diphtheria can be a skin infection or a more dangerous throat infection. It is spread by contaminated dust contacting the skin or by the inhalation of infected cough or sneeze droplets. Frequent washing and keeping the skin dry will help prevent skin infection. A vaccination is available to prevent the throat infection.

Insect Borne Diseases
Malaria This serious disease is spread by mosquito bites, and if you are travelling in endemic areas it is extremely important to take malarial prophylactics. Symptoms include headaches, fever, chills

and sweating which may subside and recur. Without treatment malaria can develop more serious, potentially fatal effects.

Malaria is probably the most serious potential health hazard a traveller will face. Although there have been many areas from which malaria has been eradicated, there are also areas where malaria is returning after eradication and malarial transmission levels have, in general, increased. This is probably because it is pretty easy to catch; a bite from an infected mosquito may result in any one of four types of malaria.

Protection against malaria means taking anti-malarial pills either daily or weekly, depending on the drug. Anti-malarial drugs do not actually prevent the disease but suppress its symptoms. Chloroquine is the normal malarial prophylactic and consists of a tablet taken once a week for two weeks prior to arrival in the infected area, weekly whilst travelling, and six weeks after you depart. Unfortunately there is a strain of malaria which is resistant to chloroquine and if you are travelling in an area infected with this strain an alternative drug is necessary. West and Central Africa, Papua New Guinea, Irian Jaya, the Solomons and Vanuatu are the most dangerous areas, but only in Central America, the Middle East and West Africa is chloroquine completely effective. Where resistance is reported you should continue to take chloroquine but supplement it with a weekly dose of Maloprim or a daily dose of Proguanil.

Chloroquine is quite safe for general use; side effects are minimal and it can be taken by pregnant women. Iroquinal/Paludine is recommended during pregnancy rather than Maloprim. Maloprim can have rare but serious side effects if the weekly dose is exceeded and some doctors recommend a check up after six months of continuous use. Fansidar, once used as a chloroquine alternative is no longer recommended as a prophylactic because of dangerous side effects, but it may still be recommended as a treatment for malaria. Chloroquine is also used for malaria treatment but in larger doses than for normal prophylaxis. Doxycycline is another anti-malarial for use where chloroquine resistance is reported; however, it causes hypersensitivity to sunlight, so extra precautions must be taken when in the sun. Precautions against being bitten should always be taken, particularly at dusk and during the night when the malaria-spreading mosquito is about.

Anti-malarials are very dangerous if taken in quantity, so if you do have a sugar-coated or tasteless variety keep them well out of your child's reach. You need a prescription for anti-malarials. Try to find a doctor who knows a bit about the disease; some doctors are uncertain of dosages or may be unaware of areas where different strains of malaria, requiring different prophylactics, are present. You should also give yourself plenty of time to get the pills as they may not be immediately available from your pharmacist. There is a liquid form of chloroquine which is much easier to administer to children and babies. Supposedly flavoured, it still tastes foul. You might have to ask your doctor for it specifically. I have had some problems finding a doctor who knew about it, and then finding a pharmacist who could make it up, but persevere, it is possible. If you can't get the syrup, opt for the weekly pill, it is much easier to do battle once a week with your child, than daily. If you decide that Sunday, for example, is malarial day, it becomes such a routine that you can't forget it.

Simply avoiding being bitten by mosquitoes will provide added protection against malaria. Mosquitoes are most active after dark and covering up as much as possible and using an insect repellent will certainly help. I always bring 'after dark clothes' which are donned at the approach of dusk. These consist of cotton long sleeved shirts and long trousers, socks and closed-in shoes. Repellent goes on all the exposed parts of the children's bodies particularly ankles, necks, faces and wrists. Sleeping clothes should also cover as much as possible. For babies you can get cotton sleeping bags which have arms and neck holes but are sewn across the bottom like a bag.

If your room has insect screens on the windows check that they're in good repair and that there are no holes for mosquitoes to enter. Taking a mosquito net is probably worthwhile, although you may not always find somewhere to hang it. Also if your child wakes up a lot in the night, you may find it hard to remember, in your befuddled state, to make sure the net is closed properly when you fall back into bed. Of course this is not so much a problem if you are sleeping under the net with your child. In areas with severe mosquito problems hotels often provide mosquito nets, 'flea bags' as Kieran called them in Africa.

A room with a fan is a good idea as mosquitoes don't like the movement of the air and if your bed is positioned under the fan they will stay away.

It is also a good idea to carry an insect spray, mosquito coils or a vaporiser. I close up the room (as much as possible) and spray it each evening before dinner. When we come back the smell, and hopefully any residue, has dispersed and any mosquitoes present are dead. Mosquito coils are useful; it is better to buy them when you arrive as they are very fragile. I always burn a coil in the bathroom overnight, unless it is well sealed, as mosquitoes congregate where it is damp.

Vaporisers are only useful where there is electric power. These small, portable gadgets vaporise insecticide tablets. They don't produce smells or smoke but the insecticide is still released into the air. If you buy one before you leave home check that it uses the appropriate voltage.

Mosquitoes are attracted by perfume, aftershave and anything dark blue in colour, so use odourless soap and toiletries.

Carry some preparation which will take the itch or sting out of insect bites. There are some good preparations and anti-histamine creams which work well. If your child suffers a lot from mosquito bites (Kieran has a strong allergic reaction where his bites look very inflamed and swell up quite alarmingly) you may find an anti-histamine medication will help. Ask your doctor or pharmacist before you leave home, although many of these preparations are available over the counter in pharmacies everywhere. Some brand names are Sudafed, Actifed, Phenergan or Benadryl. I find that when Kieran has one or two severe bites he will wake up crying and scratching several times during the night. This will occur for up to three nights when the bite finally fades. I now have a going-to-bed routine where I check Kieran after his bath, put calamine lotion on any bites and if he has some very large ones which have been bothering him during the day, I give him the required amount of anti-histamine. It reduces his reaction to the bite and helps him to sleep.

Sleeping Sickness In parts of tropical Africa tsetse flies can carry trypanosomiasis or sleeping sickness. They pass it on by biting large warm-blooded animals and are responsible for the lack of horses and cows in some areas. The tsetse fly is about twice the size of a housefly and recognisable by the scissor-like way it folds its wings when at rest. Only a small proportion of tsetse flies carry the disease but it is best to try to avoid being bitten as there is no immunisation. The flies are attracted to large moving objects, like safari buses, and to perfume or after shave and colours like dark blue.

Use a strong insect repellent (one containing 'Deet'). Swelling at the site of the bite, five or more days later, is the first sign of infection followed by fever within two to three weeks. The illness is serious but responds well to medical attention.

Dengue Fever There is no prophylactic available for this mosquito spread disease and the main preventative measure is to avoid being bitten. A sudden onset of fever, headaches and severe joint and muscle pains are the first signs before a rash starts on the trunk and spreads to the limbs and face. After a further few days, the fever will subside and recovery will begin. Serious complications are not common.

Yellow Fever This disease is endemic in many African and South American countries between 15° north and 15° south. The viral disease is transmitted to humans by mosquitoes and the initial symptoms are fever, headache, abdominal pain and vomiting. There may appear to be a brief recovery before it progresses to more severe complications including liver failure. There is no medical treatment apart from keeping the fever down and avoiding dehydration but yellow fever vaccination gives good protection for 10 years and is an entry requirement to many countries.

Chaga's Disease In remote rural areas of South and Central America this parasitic disease is transmitted by a bug which hides in crevices and palm fronds and often takes up residence in the thatched roofs of huts. It comes out to feed at night and a hard, violet-coloured swelling appears at the site of the bite in about a week. Usually the body overcomes the disease unaided but sometimes it continues and can eventually lead to death years later. Chaga's disease can be treated in its early stages but it is best to avoid thatched roof huts, sleep under a mosquito net, use insecticides and insect repellents and check for hidden insects.

Typhus Typhus is spread by ticks, mites or lice and begins as a bad cold, followed by a fever, chills, headache, muscle pains and a body rash. There is often a large painful sore at the site of the bite and nearby lymph nodes are swollen and painful.

Tick typhus is spread by ticks, and trekkers in South Africa may be at risk from cattle or wild animal ticks. Scrub typhus is spread by mites that feed on infected rodents and exists mainly in Asia and the Pacific Islands. You should take precautions if walking in rural areas in South-East Asia. Seek local advice on areas where ticks pose a danger and always check carefully for ticks after walking in a danger area. Remove any ticks with a lighted cigarette or ether. A strong insect repellent can help and serious walkers in tick areas should consider having their boots and trousers treated with benzyl benzoate and dibutyl phthalate.

Cuts, Bites & Stings

Cuts & Scratches Skin punctures can easily become infected in hot climates and may be difficult to heal. Treat any cut with an antiseptic solution and mercurochrome. Where possible avoid bandages and band-aids which can keep wounds wet. Coral cuts are notoriously slow to heal as the coral injects a weak venom into the wound. Avoid coral cuts by wearing shoes when walking on reefs and clean any coral cut thoroughly.

Make it a general rule that all cuts and grazes, no matter how insignificant they seem, are treated with mercurochrome as soon as possible. Tony and I both have experience of little scratches becoming infected wounds which took a very long time to heal. Tony actually had to have a penicillin injection, three months after the skin was broken, to cure what had been a tiny scratch.

Creams and ointments should not be used as these just keep the wound greasy and prevent it from healing. If infection does occur you could try an antibiotic powder but check that it has not passed its expiry date. Local pharmacies or first aid centres can often treat cuts, scratches or minor wounds very competently. Bathing a wound in salt water helps to clean and sterilise a wound.

Bites & Stings Bee and wasp stings are usually painful rather than dangerous. Calamine lotion gives relief, anti-histamine creams work well and ice packs will reduce the pain and swelling. See the section on malaria for information on how to avoid mosquito bites in the first place.

There are some spiders with dangerous bites but anti-venins are usually available. Scorpion stings are notoriously painful and are much more dangerous for young children and elderly people. In Mexico more people die from scorpion bites than snake bites. They often shelter in shoes or clothing.

Snake Bite To minimise the chances of being bitten always dress your child in boots, socks and long trousers when walking through undergrowth where snakes may be present. Warn your children not to put their hands into holes and crevices and to be careful when collecting firewood.

Snake bites do not cause instantaneous death and anti-venins are usually available. Keep the victim calm and still, wrap the bitten limb tightly, as you would for a sprained ankle, and then attach a splint to immobilise it. Then seek medical help. Tourniquets and sucking out the poison are now comprehensively discredited.

Bedbugs & Lice Bedbugs live in various places, particularly dirty mattresses and bedding. Spots of blood on bedclothes or on the wall around the bed can be read as a suggestion to find another hotel. Bedbugs leave itchy bites in neat rows. Calamine lotion may help.

Lice all cause itching and discomfort and make themselves at home in hair (head lice) or clothing (body lice). They get to you by direct contact with infected people or sharing combs, clothing and the like. Powder or shampoo treatment will kill the lice and infected clothing should then be washed in very hot water. Lots of children in the West bring head lice home from school and they are even more prevalent in developing countries – how often do you see people grooming each other's hair and searching for lice. Your children's contact with local children may well be closer than your own contact with the locals so be prepared. You may think it is a good idea to carry an appropriate treatment shampoo with you.

Leeches & Ticks Leeches may be present in damp rainforest conditions and attach themselves to the skin to suck the blood. Trekkers often get them on their legs or in their boots. Do not pull them off as the bite is then more likely to become infected. An insect repellent may keep them away. Salt or a lighted cigarette end will make them fall off, as will vaseline, alcohol or oil.

Jellyfish Local advice is the best way of avoiding contact with these sea creatures with their stinging tentacles. The box jellyfish found in inshore waters around northern Australia during the summer months is potentially fatal but stings from most jellyfish are simply rather painful. Dousing in vinegar will de-activate any stingers which have not 'fired'. Calamine lotion, antihistamines and analgesics may reduce the reaction and relieve the pain.

Other Sea Hazards Certain cone shells found in Australia and the Pacific can give a dangerous or even fatal sting. There are various fish and other sea creatures which can give dangerous stings or bites or which are dangerous to eat. Again local advice is the best suggestion.

Travellers' Tales

SOUTH AMERICA & MEXICO

SOUTH AMERICA

Our first visit to South America was made in early '85 when Tashi was four and Kieran just two. In fact we scheduled our departure date so Kieran got on the plane a one year old 10% traveller, and woke up the next morning in Peru age two! We had about five weeks travelling time and we stuck to the Andean countries – Peru, Bolivia and Ecuador.

Our children were still very young travellers at this time so it wasn't the easiest trip we've ever made but, as usual, there was plenty to see and do and some memorable moments. In fact there were some moments we'd rather not remember – there was one lunch time restaurant meal in Trujillo where every possible combination of the old equation children plus restaurant equals disaster came up. We eventually had to leave a very large tip and slink out as quietly as possible leaving broken glasses, spilt soup, tipped over chairs and other assorted debris behind us. Usually, however, the trip was far smoother and a great deal more fun.

In Cuzco, llamas and the colourful people of the Peruvian highlands were a constant attraction. There's a distinct travellers' feel, much like Kathmandu in Nepal, about this ancient Inca capital and lots of interesting little restaurants and cafes to try quite apart from the many things to see in and around the town. Folk singers, wandering from cafe to cafe in the evening, were another big hit with the children.

The train trip to Machu Picchu (our two were far too young to contemplate walking the Inca Trail at this time) is the big excursion from Cuzco and we stayed a night there and enjoyed having the site almost to ourselves early the next morning. On

the way back we stopped overnight at Ollantaytambo, a delightful small town with more ancient Inca ruins overlooking it. Another overnight trip from Cuzco took us to nearby Pisac with more Inca ruins – this time way up high on the mountainside overlooking the town, and a colourful and interesting Sunday market.

Altitude problems are always possible in these Andean towns and with children, who may not be able to tell you what is wrong, it's a particular worry. We had a couple of worried nights with Kieran in Cuzco but it turned out to be insect bites (insects love to nibble him) rather than anything to do with the altitude. When we continued by train to Puno on Lake Titicaca we really felt the height, however. At 3820 metres the air there is very thin and when the kids got exhausted we certainly didn't have much energy to pick them up and trudge on. Fortunately all over town there are men pushing small trolleys to transport goods from place to place and on a couple of occasions we hired one of these and had our children transported instead!

We continued to Bolivia from Puno but our visit there was a brief one as the country's interminable series of revolutions seemed about to add another to the list and almost everything was on strike. The currency was also falling through the floor, the banks were shut and it really wasn't worth changing more than US$20 at a time because you couldn't conveniently carry more than that in Bolivian notes! We've got a photo of Tashi carrying what looks like a large stack of Monopoly money; it's actually just US$20 worth of seriously devalued local currency.

From Bolivia we continued back to Peru and on to Ecuador where we enjoyed bustling Quito, relaxing Baños, a harrowing bus ride down from the Andes to the coast and then flew out to the Galapagos Islands, one of the highlights of the trip. It's unfortunate that Kieran was so young at the time as I'm sure that a few years later, with his natural history mania in full flow, he would have enjoyed this trip as much as the Africa trip we made four years later. Never mind, there were animals aplenty from giant tortoises to friendly seals, and huge lizards to colourful blue footed boobies.

Finally we made our way back down the coast of Peru to Lima, spent a few days more in that troubled but interesting city and then flew back to North America. It hadn't been a totally easy trip; the distances even in these smaller Andean countries are often great and the travel can be slow. Plus our children were still very young for serious travelling, but we'd go back there in a flash.

Tony Wheeler

MEXICO

We went to Mexico with the children in '87 when Tashi was six and Kieran three. We rarely plan our trips very thoroughly or do too much booking ahead and on this occasion it actually backfired on us slightly. Our intention was to fly straight to the south (to Cancun on the Yucatan Peninsula), rent a car immediately and set off into the Yucatan, then work our way back toward the US.

Unfortunately arriving on New Year's Day without a place booked to stay was not a wise idea and our first couple of days getting on our feet seemed to be one long hotel hunt. Thereafter, however, we never had trouble finding a room, the crush seemed to extend no further than 2 January! A few days into the trip we turned up at one place where, lesson learnt, we had booked a room, only to find they were full up and had no record of our booking whatsoever. We managed to find somewhere else in the small town but ever afterwards if we have booked a room Tashi will ask, just as we turn up, 'do you think they'll have the room for us, or will this be like Mexico?' Mexico is going to go down in our family history as the place where bookings don't get made!

Those early problems apart we had a terrific time. There were pleasant beaches along the Caribbean and Pacific coasts. The enormous variety of Mayan and Aztec ruins could have been terminally boring for the kids but in actual fact so many of the great pyramids are like super climbing equipment that our two seemed to spend far too much time bounding up one side and down the other to get bored. Even the many museums, and Mexico has some truly superb museums, always seemed to have plenty of exhibits to amuse children. The terrific exhibit of dancing skeletons and other Day of the Dead creations at the Museo Regional de Artesanias in Mérida went down very well.

And there was lots of excitement and fun. The La Quebrada

divers at Acapulco were just as thrilling as they're supposed to be. A group of street mime artists we saw one night in the Zona Rosa in Mexico City were a big hit. The ruins at Monte Albàn near Oaxaca were enlivened by some friendly donkeys while the El Rey ruins near Cancun had huge lizards. A celebration in the village of San Juan Chamula near San Cristòbal de las Casas was enlivened by a constant barrage of fireworks and skyrockets.

Mexico is a wonderful place for craft shopping and, as on a number of trips to Bali, one of the real pleasures of travelling with children came at departure time when we had four people's baggage allowances to use up! Mexico proved irresistible to small shoppers as well. Kieran was going through a *Master of the Universe* craze at that time and the small plastic figures he avidly collected were made in Mexico, on view in every toy shop window we passed by and about a quarter of the price of back home. He ensured there was going to be no way we could pass up such an obvious bargain!

The street life in the older colonial-style towns was a delight. Several times we got big, comfortable old rooms overlooking the *zocalo*, the main square of the town. We could sit out on our balcony for hours watching life go on below us. A day's sightseeing could end with a stroll around the square, followed by a beer for the adults and an ice cream for the kids at some sidewalk cafe.

Our time was too limited and the distances too great to do much bus travel – we flew a lot – but the bus trips we did make were no problem. Mexico was a wonderful place to travel.

Tony Wheeler

Travelling Pregnant

The day before Tony and I left for India to research our India book, I discovered I was pregnant. Since I obviously knew it was a possibility I had decided that I would continue with the trip, despite the fact that I had had a miscarriage a few months before. Now some may think I was/am crazy; I can live with that. I guess that it comes down to your own personal philosophy: I don't think I was irresponsible, because I did not feel that going to India would increase my chances of miscarrying again. I knew India well, and I was quite aware of what I was letting myself in for. I also knew how to minimise the hassles, I was healthy, I intended to be careful and beyond that I really wanted to go. While I was quite aware that a child was going to radically change my life, I was not prepared to start compromising before it was even born! I knew that after the baby was born I would still want to travel, so I felt that travelling with this small internal passenger was an entirely appropriate beginning.

When to Travel

The first three months of a pregnancy are the most risky; however, the first three months may be the best time to travel in that you are not too big, you don't get quite so tired and you may be more able emotionally to handle the problems you may encounter while travelling. Unless you suffer from 'morning sickness' you may not feel too much different from 'normal' and really enjoy your last trip as a non-parent!

The final three months also pose some health risks and it is wise to be reasonably close to medical help during this time. This is also the time when your greater size makes you most tired and uncomfortable. Airlines have regulations regarding the last few weeks of pregnancy when they can refuse to carry you.

Be Prepared

Before you organise your trip, read up all you can on pregnancy and health. Find a sympathetic doctor, preferably one who has travelled or deals with travellers and ask their advice, and know about vaccinations and suitable medications for the ailments you are likely to be exposed to. Read about the countries you are going to and choose your route carefully. It is easier if it is a country you have already visited, or if you are an experienced traveller.

Ask yourself if you are prepared to take the responsibility (and the flak!) if things go wrong – the risk is yours.

Food

Almost anywhere you travel it is possible to get good, healthy food, although in some places well off the beaten track you may find it difficult to maintain a balanced diet or, particularly in places like India, the food may be so over cooked that little nutrition remains. In many Third World countries dairy foods are not always available. It is important to maintain a good diet, so I would suggest that you upgrade your standard of restaurant whenever you feel it is necessary. Eat eggs, fruit and other available foods, and try not to miss meals or wait too long between meals. Peanuts are also good as a source of protein and are generally available. Read up on the properties of food and know what you need and how to meet your needs.

Chinese restaurants seem to be found in even the most remote places in the Third World and their food is generally good. In India dhal, a lentil soup which is a good source of protein, is almost always served with meals, or you can also ask for it. An Indian *thali* of rice, dhal, vegetables and yoghurt is completely adequate. Yoghurt (*dahi* or 'curd') is often available if you ask, you can also drink it as *lassi*.

Supplements

Carry multi-vitamins, iron tablets and calcium tablets, and check with your doctor (who will advise you to stay home) or a health food store as to the most appropriate.

Other Considerations

Besides the medical considerations, in the first three months of pregnancy you will be surprised at three things:

How hungry you get. Tony used to be amazed at my capacity for lousy Indian food. No matter how tasteless or awful it was, I ate mine, Tony's and anyone else's. If you miss a meal due to travelling by train or bus or arriving late you may feel sick or even faint, so always carry something you can eat with you, and snack on fruit, peanuts – anything you can find to keep you going. You do need it.

How tired you get. Don't try to do all the things you did before you got pregnant. Take frequent rests. If you have one day of hard travel, have a day or two of rest and just plan to travel at a slower pace.

How often you will need to find a toilet. Your bladder will be uncomfortable more often than you thought possible. It's wise to dress for quick and convenient toilet visits.

You may find that travelling on a bus or train for many hours at a stretch makes your back ache. I found taking off and landing by plane also caused my lower back to ache. I met a doctor who was on the same flight to Leh and asked her what might be causing this. She thought it was probably caused by changes in pressure, and since it hadn't caused any real problems so far, it was probably all right.

If you are prone to motion sickness, you should consider trying to avoid it by limiting your trips on vehicles that make you sick, particularly if you actually vomit since it is not a good idea for pregnant women to be violently sick. Check with your doctor if there is a safe medication you can take to prevent motion sickness or try the 'ginger treatment'; ie, a capsule of ginger before you travel.

Really, you have to take the same precautions you would if you stayed at home. Just be aware of any extra problems you might meet, and be prepared to take the responsibility if anything goes wrong – everyone will think you are crazy!

TRAVEL HEALTH
Vaccinations
The first hassle is the vaccinations. Pregnant women should not take drugs nor be given 'live vaccines' and, of course, if you plan to travel to some areas you must have certain vaccinations and take anti-malarials. See the health section for which vaccinations are safe for pregnant women.

If at all possible, if you are planning to become pregnant and you know you may be travelling, try to get all the immunisations you need before you get pregnant. Due to the limited periods of immunity afforded by many vaccinations this may not be practical, but at least consider it.

Diarrhoea
Try not to take any unnecessary medication. If you get diarrhoea, try to clear it up with rest and a bland diet. If you can't get rid of it use a kaolin preparation (available from most chemists in the West). Lomotil is contra-indicated in pregnancy but if you do want to carry something with you for diarrhoea check with your doctor first. I was extra careful when I was travelling in India during my first pregnancy and didn't get sick at all. I think prevention is much better than taking something in this instance.

Malaria
This disease can pass from the mother through the placenta to the foetus. If a mother contracts malaria during pregnancy her baby can be born with malaria. A pregnant woman is likely to have malaria far more seriously than the non-pregnant.

Some anti-malarial drugs, in particular chloroquine, are considered safe to take during pregnancy but others may have known side-effects or may not yet be sufficiently tested. Get advice from your doctor or health authorities as to which drug is most suitable for you. The health chapter gives the current thinking on malarials for pregnant women.

Minor Problems

Yeast and fungal infections can be a problem for the pregnant woman. Infections of the vagina are common in pregnant women anywhere, but if you are travelling in the tropics the hot climate exacerbates the problem. Cotton underwear, not too tight, is absolutely essential. Don't wear jeans or trousers too much; loose cotton dresses are better. Carry a preparation to cure the problem if it arises – again check with your doctor for an appropriate one.

Travellers' Tales

AFRICA

In 1989 we made our first trip to Africa; the children were eight and five. It was a straightforward visit with the intention of doing the most straightforwardly touristy thing – ie, to see the wildlife – and it was an all round success. We only went to two countries, as that was all our six weeks would allow, starting and finishing in Zimbabwe (the gateway to Africa from Australia) but spending most of our time in Kenya (sub-Saharan Africa's big tourist attraction).

We'd booked hotels for the first couple of nights in both countries and in Kenya at least it turned out to be a very good idea as our Zimbabwe-Kenya flight was endlessly delayed and we arrived in Nairobi from the airport after 1 am – not a good time to be looking for a hotel in a strange town with two children in tow. We had our fingers crossed that this wouldn't be one of those occasions where nobody had heard of our reservation, but everything was fine.

It only took a couple of hours in Nairobi to organise a safari. The city is positively thronged with safari minibuses coming and going from the superb Kenyan wildlife reserves so it's no problem at all to find one going where you want to go and when you want to go. We thought a visit to the two major reserves, Amboseli and Masai Mara, would be the ideal, split by a spell on the beach so the children didn't suffer wildlife overload.

So a couple of days after arriving we set off with a small American/Australian party for Amboseli on a camping safari with Best Camping. Kenyan safaris come in a wide range from all out luxury down to 'cheap and cheerful' camping; Best are down at the cheap and cheerful end of the range. That means

143

about US$30 per person (half price for kids) including all your park entry fees, transport, game drives, camping equipment, food and so on. We thought it was great value and the trip turned out to be just what we wanted – camping out at night, eating around the fire, with animals off in the undergrowth.

The only catch was that the animals didn't always play their part and stay off in the undergrowth. Having baboons scavenging around the campsite wasn't too bad but a herd of elephants strolling through at night does not help you to sleep easily! The kids were really rather frightened when one elephant decided to have a look at what was being served for dinner (we're all still here so the saying that they know not to step on tents must be true!).

We concluded our camping safari at Amboseli and Tsavo West with a night of luxury at the wonderful *Kilaguni Lodge*. Instead of chasing the wildlife around you sit and wait for the animals to come to the water hole in front of the lodge, which they certainly do at all hours of the night and day. From there we took a *matatu*, the local public minibuses, down to the old town of Mombasa on the coast then flew in a light aircraft north to the ancient Swahili Arab trading port of Lamu.

We didn't even have to look for a place to stay in Lamu because a house owner found us on the ferry over from the airport and rented us his traditional old house, complete with houseboy for about US$40 a day. We lounged around the house, went sailing on *dhows*, visited ancient ruins and fell in love with this colourful old town. It's a place with an atmosphere that visitors to places like Kathmandu or Cuzco will find instantly recognisable. Having the house was great – Tashi and Kieran really made themselves at home there – and the whole town, where donkeys are still the normal transport and the district commissioner's Land-Rover is the sole motor vehicle, is wonderful to wander about with children.

From Lamu we headed back towards Mombasa with a few

days pause at the beach resort of Malindi. Again we had a good place to stay and here the children got themselves involved in a game that continued with undiminished interest for the rest of our trip. A barman at the hotel (Tashi and Kieran love propping up bars!) showed them how the plastic insert in Coke and Fanta bottle caps pulled out and had an African animal head on the back. There was some sort of quest to find six different animals one of which had to be a rhino. But that was unimportant to our two – for them it was simply a matter of finding as many as possible of as many different kinds as possible. You didn't even have to buy the drinks; bottle caps were littered around every soft drinks stand, restaurant or bus stand!

From Mombasa we took the wonderful old overnight train back to Nairobi (but forget about the food which is decidedly unexceptional) and set about organising another safari. This time it was to Masai Mara and instead of a camping safari we stayed in a 'tented camp', which seemed to mean something that looked slightly like it might be a tent but was set up permanently. The site, *Cottar's Mara Camp*, was quite delightful and the sheer variety and numbers of animals in the Mara was just knockout. Our only regret was we had not made the visit to the Mara a longer one.

The camp also provided the trip's most amusing incident with some much smaller African wildlife. Just before bedtime one night a largish spider made its way over the ceiling above the kids' beds. I pulled a chair over, climbed up and trapped it in a glass held against the ceiling. I then needed a card or piece of paper to cap the glass but before anybody could pass it up my sarong fell off, leaving me standing stark naked on a chair, holding a glass against the ceiling. Fortunately nobody did look in the open door to our cabin for the next few minutes as Maureen and the children were laughing far too hard to pass me the necessary spider catching equipment. Well you should always strip down to catch African spiders I insisted later, that way there's no chance of them falling down inside your shirt.

Back in Nairobi we spent one night and then set off on our third safari. This time we rented a car and drove ourselves and stayed in regular lodges at Lake Nakura and Lake Baringo. At these parks it's the birdlife (in particular the millions of flamingos at Nakura) which is the big attraction, but there were plenty of animals as well. Finally it was back to Nairobi again with a final day around the town's outskirts including

the Nairobi National Park, where we saw those elusive rhino again, and a visit to the giraffe sanctuary, where the opportunity to climb up on a platform and hand feed a giraffe was a big hit.

Our African visit was a major success with the children; this is a vacation that is a long way from an adults-only activity. We rarely suffered wildlife overload and the often long hours in safari minibuses didn't cause any major problems. With Kieran in particular the visit seems to have had an ongoing effect, he has become positively fanatical about African wild-life and an instant expert on telling a wildebeest from a buffalo, a waterbuck from a hartebeest or a Thomson's gazelle from an impala. We've even had to make a visit to the zoo at home soon after returning, just to keep in touch.

Tony Wheeler

The safaris were the highlight of our trip to Africa. No child can fail to be excited and thrilled at seeing these magnificent animals in their natural habitat, and adults feel the same way. One of our contributors has taken her children, aged two and three years old and had a wonderful experience, although the older they are obviously the more they will get out of it.

If you are travelling by minibus you don't have to worry so much about the sun but it is worthwhile having a small crushable cap or hat you can easily stuff in your bag for the occasions when you leave the vehicle. Sunglasses are useful for when the sun is glaring through the windows of the bus. Take insect repellent, particularly on dusk drives, to protect against mosquitoes, but you should apply it all the time as tsetse flies may enter the bus. If you are in an open vehicle, sunscreen, a shady hat and long cotton pants and long-sleeved shirts are necessary.

Carry something to drink and a few nibbles for when the children are tired and perhaps an animal hasn't appeared for a while. I had some powder for flavouring water which was very useful, and I also carried some peanut butter, and Milo which I added to their milk. This was really worth having on the nights when the children didn't fancy the camp fare.

For younger children it may be useful to carry a game or book to while away the periods when the animals don't co-operate. Our children were perfectly happy with a spotters' guide and I recommend you buy a good comprehensive one as they are invaluable. Everyone should have their own pair of binoculars as you don't want to be arguing over whose turn it is for the only pair when a lion appears! Although we bought a small, light set mainly for the children, they managed the larger pairs just as easily. Give the children lessons on using them and make sure they are adept before you hit the game parks.

A few games or drawing/colouring materials are useful for when you are in camp, Kieran's' prized possession became a little stuffed lion he had brought with him and some wooden animals he bought on Lamu.

A good sunscreen is essential, and eye lotion or drops are a good idea for applying after a days' dusty drive. As well as light cotton clothes for the day, carry something warm for the evenings which can be surprisingly cold. At night use a strong insect repellent and take the usual precautions to keep off mosquitoes.

If you are going on a safari with a group of strangers, it is important to impress upon your children how they should behave. This safari is probably as much a thrill of a lifetime for the others, and whining or noisy children will not be welcome. Choose your safari with care, the fewer the people the more manageable it may be. Keep your children under your supervision and join in with the others on all the usual camp tasks. We met lovely people who enjoyed our children as much as the children enjoyed them, but you might not be so lucky. The safari companies don't really cater for children as such – there are many more adults than children on the trips – so it's up to you to take care of your kids.

Maureen Wheeler

Swaziland

This is an excellent country to take children to and we always look forward to our trips there. Being almost in the highlands (the small area of low veldt excepted), Swaziland rarely gets oppressively hot and the temperature is generally equivalent to a warm English summers' day. During the monsoon months (October to March) there is quite a bit of rainfall but lots of sunny days in between.

There are several supermarkets in Swaziland in which you can buy everything you need for your child in the line of food, toys and clothes – even safe, pasteurised milk! Mbabane and Manzine also have extensive shopping centres with every type of shop and reasonably priced goods. There are several things to do with your children in Swaziland and it is so small that all forms of entertainment are easily accessible. Several hotels in Swaziland have excellent swimming pools where you can usually swim for the price of a drink. There is also a wonderful swimming pool filled with warm filtered water from a hot springs. As well as being good therapy for your aches and pains the 'Cuddle Puddle', as it is called, is a great favourite with all children, especially on cloudy or rainy days when other swimming pools are too cold.

Swaziland does not boast any really spectacular wildlife, but there is plenty to keep the average child happy. There are two game parks: Milwaree, in the Ezulwini Valley, has zebras, warthogs, monkeys, impala, wildebeest, ostrich, the odd giraffe, hippo and a croc; Malololcha has some of the same animals in the more spectacular surroundings. There are also nature reserves, notably the Phophonyane Nature Reserve which has beautiful riverside trails and some spectacular waterfalls to clamber near, but not over – I fell down one of these waterfalls while pregnant with my third child; luckily she emerged three months later unscathed by her bumpy ride.

Nearly all the large hotels have playgrounds and so does the main park in Mbabane. There are several craft centres and markets between Manzini and Mbabane. Notable favourites with our children were Mantenga Crafts (by Mantenga Hotel), where there is also a small cafe and sometimes monkeys; Tishweshwe Crafts (Malkerns) which also has a cafe with good cake and fine views over pineapple fields; and Indighilizi Gallery (Mbabane) which has some lovely crafts and good exhibitions.

Accommodation in Swaziland is generally good and there are several motel-type places which often have self catering facilities.

Zimbabwe

Zimbabwe is an easy African country to travel with children; you can find everything you need in the major towns of Zimbabwe and most things elsewhere. They make almost everything themselves so nothing is quite like its western equivalent, but is an adequate substitute. The major hotels have swimming pools and there are playparks in most cities and often attached to the larger hotels. Hwange Game Park is definitely worth visiting and there are several lodges which are suitable for children both inside and outside the park.

Other attractions are the Kariba Dam, which is interesting, instructive and impressive. The surrounding craft centres and African village also appeal to children. Victoria Falls is also very impressive; there are several walking trails which are quite manageable with children. The nearby crocodile farm is very well organised and you get to hold a baby croc. The trips down the Zambezi River are good as you see hippos and crocs, and the cave paintings outside Bulowayo in the Matopos Hills are well worth visiting.

Tanzania

Tanzania is a more difficult country to take children to, as it is very hot, humid by the coast and being a socialist country has very little in the way of western foods or goods. However the game viewing is spectacular and there are some picturesque beaches that are well worth visiting.

Basic fruits and vegetables, rice and a kind of maize meal (mealy maize) which is the staple diet are available. Meat and bread are difficult to get hold of.

The main attraction in Tanzania is its wildlife. The most famous parks are Serengetti, Ngorogoro Crater and Lake Manyara, all in central Tanzania. You fly to Arushia and from there it is a six hour drive along unsealed road to the main game areas. It sounds daunting but there is lots to see on the way, including the spectacular Masai people. Our children were two and three years old and were carried along by our enthusiasm so that everyone found it a thrilling experience.

Two other game parks worth mentioning are: Mikumi (about five hours from Dar by car), where there is plenty of wildlife and a lodge which is very adequate and suitable for children, and Selous Game Reserve, a very remote and more primitive game reserve. You feel that you are really in the wilds here and it is most inspiring; accommodation is scanty but adequate.

Philippa Freeland

Index

Africa 143-151
  Safaris 147-148
  Swaziland 149, 150
  Tanzania 151
  Zimbabwe 150
Altitude Sickness 118
Asian Children 18-19
Australia 26-30

Babies 11, 18, 35
Babysitters 21-22
Backpacks 57-58
Bali 61-64
Bathing 77-78
Bedbugs 131-132
Bedding 75-76
Bicycles 56-57
Bilharzia 125
Bites 131
Breast Feeding 79-80

Chaga's Disease 130
Cheap Hotels 22
Children 11, 35
China 97-103
Chloroquine 126
Cholera 121
Clothes 69-70
Cook Islands 33-34
Cots 75-76
Culture Shock 19
Cuts 130-131

Dengue Fever 129
Diarrhoea 119-120
Diphtheria 125
Doxycycline 126
Drinking 81

Dysentery 121

Eating 82-90
  Babies 89
  Baby Formula 88
  Camping Stove 87
  Children 89
  Dairy Products 88
  Markets 87
  Restaurants 84
  Room Service 86

Fever 113-114
Flying 35-51
  Airlines 38
  Airports 38-39
  Babies 35, 44
  Baggage Allowance 36-37
  Bassinets 39, 45
  Children's Meals 38
  Clothing 49-50
  Fares 36
  Food 43-44
  Nappies 40
  Older Kids 35, 45
  Pre-boarding 38
  Seating 46-47
  Sedation 47
  Sleeping 45-46
  Special Diets 39
  Take-off (& Landing) 50
  Time Zones 51
  Toddlers 35
  Toys 41
Food 79-82
Fungal Infections 116-117

Gastroenteritis 121-122

Giardia 120-121

Health Guides 104
Health Insurance 104-105
Health Precautions 108-112
Heat Exhaustion 116
Heat Stroke 116
Hepatitis 122
Hong Kong 93
Hypothermia 117-118

India 68
Indonesia 65-66

Japan 91-96
Jellyfish 132
Junk Food 24

Language 17, 21
Leeches 132
Lice 131-132
Local Transport 56
Long Distance Transport 52
    Buses 52
    Taxis 54
    Train 53

Macau 93
Malaria 125-129
Maloprim 126
Medical Kit 105-106
Meningitis 124
Mexico 136-137
Milk 82
Money 22
Mosquitoes 127-129
Motion Sickness 48-49, 118-119

Nappies 70-72
Nepal 67-68
New Zealand 31-32
Nutrition 109-110

Passports 10-11
People 15, 16

Phenergan 47
Poverty 20
Pregnancy 138-151
    Diarrhoea 141
    Food 139
    Fungal Infections 141
    Malaria 141
    Vaccinations 141
    Vitamin Supplements 139
Prickly Heat 115-116
Proguanil 126

Rabies 123-124
Rehydration 119-120
Rent-a-Cars 54-55
    Chauffeurs 55
    Infant Seats 54-55
    Safety Belts 54-55
Respiration 111
Room Service 24

Scratches 130-131
Self Diagnosis 112-113
Sleeping 71-74
Sleeping Sickness 129
Snake Bite 131
South America 133-136
Sri Lanka 68
Stings 131
Strollers 57-58
Sunburn 114-115
Swimming 17

Tantrums 18
Temperature 111
Tetanus 123
Ticks 132
Toddlers 11,18, 35
Toilets 78-79
Travelling 23-24
Treatment 112-113
Trekking 58-60
    Porters 58
    Protection 59
Tuberculosis 124-125

Typhoid 122-123
Typhus 130

Vaccinations 106-108
  Cholera 107
  Diptheria 107-108
  Hepatitis 108
  Meningitis 108
  Smallpox 107
  Tetanus 107

Typhoid 108
  Yellow Fever 108
Visas 11

Walking (see Trekking)
Water 81
Water Purification 110-111
Worms 123

Yellow Fever 129

Temperature

To convert °C to °F multiply by 1.8 and add 32

To convert °F to °C subtract 32 and multiply by ·55

Length, Distance & Area

	multiply by
inches to centimetres	2.54
centimetres to inches	0.39
feet to metres	0.30
metres to feet	3.28
yards to metres	0.91
metres to yards	1.09
miles to kilometres	1.61
kilometres to miles	0.62
acres to hectares	0.40
hectares to acres	2.47

Weight

	multiply by
ounces to grams	28.35
grams to ounces	0.035
pounds to kilograms	0.45
kilograms to pounds	2.21
British tons to kilograms	1016
US tons to kilograms	907

A British ton is 2240 lbs, a US ton is 2000 lbs

Volume

	multiply by
Imperial gallons to litres	4.55
litres to imperial gallons	0.22
US gallons to litres	3.79
litres to US gallons	0.26

5 imperial gallons equals 6 US gallons
a litre is slightly more than a US quart, slightly less
than a British one

Lonely Planet Publications

Lonely Planet is known to travellers around the world for its unique range of travel guides. Lonely Planet travel guides are written for travellers who want to explore beyond the normal tourist routes and are written with an emphasis on practical, down-to-earth information.

Since the early '70s well over a million travellers have read these guides, used them, shared them, loved them, abused them, traded them and written letters to help update them.

The Lonely Planet list includes guides to virtually every accessible part of Asia, as well as Australia, the Pacific, Central and South America, Africa and parts of North America. The information is constantly updated and revised editions are published on a two-year cycle.

All Lonely Planet books are designed for constant use, with quality paper, laminated covers and strong smyth-sewn binding so they will last for thousands of miles out on the road.

Shoestring Guides
Compact, essential information for low-budget travel in a major region or continent.

Travel survival kits
In-depth coverage of a single country or small group of countries for a range of budgets.

Walking guides
Information on some of the world's most fascinating regions and details on the most exciting walking routes.

Language survival kits
Practical phrasebooks with essential words and phrases that cover day-to-day travelling situations.

And also. . .
Lonely Planet publications include advice for travelling with children, a cartoonist's travels and a newsletter.

A selection of guides from Lonely Planet

Australia – a travel survival kit
Australia is Lonely Planet's home territory so this guide gives you the complete low-down on Down Under, from the red centre to the coast, from cosmopolitan cities to country towns.

Canada – a travel survival kit
Canada offers a unique combination of French, English and American culture in a vast country of forests, mountains and lakes.

India – a travel survival kit
An award-winning guidebook that is recognised as the outstanding contemporary guide to the subcontinent. Looking for a houseboat in Kashmir? Trying to post a parcel? This definitive guidebook has all the facts.

Thailand – a travel survival kit
Beyond the Buddhist temples and Bangkok bars there is much to see in fascinating Thailand. This extensively researched guide presents an inside look at Thailand's culture, people and language.

China – a travel survival kit
Travelling on your own in China can be exciting and rewarding; it can also be exhausting and frustrating – getting a seat on a train or finding a cheap bed in a hotel isn't always easy. But it can be done and this detailed and comprehensive book tells you how.

South-East Asia on a shoestring
For over 10 years this has been known as the 'yellow bible' to travellers in South-East Asia. It has all the latest information on Brunei, Burma Hong Kong, Indonesia, Macau, Malaysia, Papua New Guinea, the Philippines, Singapore, and Thailand.

Trekking in the Nepal Himalaya
Complete trekking information for Nepal, including day-by-day route descriptions and detailed maps – this book has a wealth of advice for both independent and group trekkers.

Lonely Planet Guidebooks

Lonely Planet guidebooks cover virtually every accessible part of Asia as well as Australia, the Pacific, Central and South America, Africa, the Middle East and parts of North America. There are four main series: 'travel survival kits', covering a single country for a range of budgets; 'shoestring' guides with compact information for low-budget travel in a major region; trekking guides; and 'phrasebooks'.

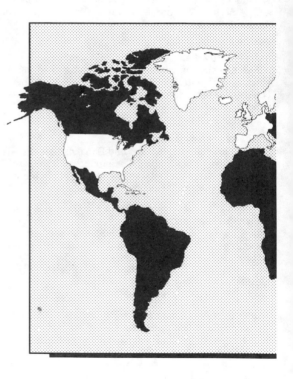

Australia & the Pacific
Australia
Bushwalking in Australia
Papua New Guinea
Papua New Guinea phrasebook
New Zealand
Tramping in New Zealand
Rarotonga & the Cook Islands
Solomon Islands
Tahiti & French Polynesia
Fiji
Micronesia
Tonga
Samoa

South-East Asia
South-East Asia on a shoestring
Malaysia, Singapore & Brunei
Indonesia
Bali & Lombok
Indonesia phrasebook
Burma
Burmese phrasebook
Thailand
Thai phrasebook
Philippines
Pilipino phrasebook

North-East Asia
North-East Asia on a shoestring
China
China phrasebook
Tibet
Tibet phrasebook
Japan
Japanese phrasebook
Korea
Korean phrasebook
Hong Kong, Macau & Canton
Taiwan

West Asia
West Asia on a shoestring
Trekking in Turkey
Turkey

Indian Ocean
Madagascar & Comoros
Mauritius, Réunion & Seychelles
Maldives & Islands of the East Indian Ocean

Mail Order

Lonely Planet guidebooks are distributed worldwide and are sold by good bookshops everywhere. They are also available by mail order from Lonely Planet, so if you have difficulty finding a title please write to us. US and Canadian residents should write to Embarcadero West, 112 Linden St, Oakland CA 94607, USA and residents of other countries to PO Box 617, Hawthorn, Victoria 3122, Australia.

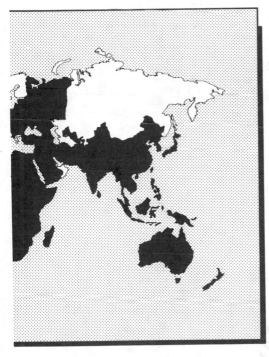

Eastern Europe
Eastern Europe

Indian Subcontinent
India
Hindi/Urdu phrasebook
Kashmir, Ladakh & Zanskar
Trekking in the Indian Himalaya
Pakistan
Kathmandu & the Kingdom of Nepal
Trekking in the Nepal Himalaya
Nepal phrasebook
Sri Lanka
Sri Lanka phrasebook
Bangladesh
Karakoram Highway

Africa
Africa on a shoestring
East Africa
Swahili phrasebook
West Africa
Central Africa
Morocco, Algeria & Tunisia

North America
Canada
Alaska

Mexico
Mexico
Baja California

South America
South America on a shoestring
Ecuador & the Galapagos Islands
Colombia
Chile & Easter Island
Bolivia
Brazil
Peru
Argentina
Quechua phrasebook

Middle East
Israel
Egypt & the Sudan
Jordan & Syria
Yemen

Lonely Planet

Lonely Planet published its first book in 1973. Tony and Maureen Wheeler had made a lengthy overland trip from England to Australia and, in response to numerous 'how do you do it?' questions, Tony wrote and they published *Across Asia on the Cheap*. It became an instant local best-seller and inspired thoughts of a second travel guide. A year and a half in South-East Asia resulted in their second book, *South-East Asia on a Shoestring*, which they put together in a backstreet Chinese hotel in Singapore in 1975. The 'yellow book', as it quickly became known, soon became *the* guide to the region and has gone through five editions, always with its familiar yellow cover.

Soon other writers came to them with ideas for similar books – books that went off the beaten track with an adventurous approach to travel, books that 'assumed you knew how to get your luggage off the carousel,' as one reviewer put it. Lonely Planet grew from a kitchen table operation to a spare room and then to its own office. Its international reputation began to grow as the Lonely Planet logo began to appear in more and more countries. In 1982 *India – a travel survival kit* won the Thomas Cook award for the best guidebook of the year.

These days there are over 70 Lonely Planet titles. Over 40 people work at our office in Melbourne, Australia and another half dozen at our US office in Oakland, California.

At first Lonely Planet specialised in the Asia region but these days we are also developing major ranges of guidebooks to the Pacific region, to South America and to Africa. The list of walking guides is growing and Lonely Planet now has a unique series of phrasebooks to 'unusual' languages. The emphasis continues to be on travel for travellers and Tony and Maureen still manage to fit in a number of trips each year and play a very active part in the writing and updating of Lonely Planet's guides.

Keeping guidebooks up to date is a constant battle which requires an ear to the ground and lots of walking, but technology also plays its part. All Lonely Planet guidebooks are now stored and updated on computer, and some authors even take lap-top computers into the field. Lonely Planet is also using computers to draw maps and eventually many of the maps will be stored on disk.

The people at Lonely Planet strongly feel that travellers can make a positive contribution to the countries they visit both by better appreciation of cultures and by the money they spend. In addition the company tries to make a direct contribution to the countries and regions it covers. Since 1986 a percentage of the income from each book has gone to aid groups and associations. This has included donations to famine relief in Africa, to aid projects in India, to agricultural projects in Central America, to Greenpeace's efforts to halt French nuclear testing in the Pacific and to Amnesty International. In 1989 $41,000 was donated by Lonely Planet to these projects.
